KU-486-612

CONTENTS

ACKNOWLEDGEMENTS

Thanks are due to the various Preservation Societies in the county, also the many libraries in the area who gave valuable assistance. Thanks also go to Chris Turner and Rod Blencowe for finding many early Lens of Sutton pictures, and to Arthur Tayler, John H. Meredith, John F. Bradshaw, Paul Bolger of Stations UK, Folkestone Library, Elizabeth Straupmanis of Gravesham Borough Council, Regeneration Section and the Ironbridge Gorge Museum Trust.

Personal thanks go to Anthony Rispoli, railway photographer, who provided the majority of the current Kent pictures as well as supplying much information, to Brian Butler who provided the maps for the original 1988 *Kent Railways Remembered* book and to Joan, my wife, who gave invaluable help in making this book possible.

LOST RAILWAYS
OF KENT

Leslie Oppitz

COUNTRYSIDE BOOKS
NEWBURY, BERKSHIRE

First published 2003
© Leslie Oppitz 2003

COUNTRYSIDE BOOKS
3 Catherine Road
Newbury, Berkshire

To view our complete range of books,
please visit us at
www.countrysidebooks.co.uk

ISBN 1 85306 803 9

The cover picture shows 'Schools' class locomotive no 30918
Hurstpierpoint hauling a London-bound express train past
Shakespeare Cliff in the late 1950s. The locomotive was
withdrawn in October 1961.
(From an original painting by Colin Doggett)

Typeset by Textype, Cambridge
Produced through MRM Associates Ltd., Reading
Printed by Woolnough Bookbinding Ltd., Irthlingborough

ABBREVIATIONS

The following abbreviations are used in this book:

CWR	Canterbury & Whitstable Railway
CTRL	Channel Tunnel Rail Link
DEMU	Diesel Electric Multiple Unit
EKLR	East Kent Light Railway
EKR	East Kent Railway (to become LCDR from 1859)
EVLR	Elham Valley Light Railway
KESR	Kent & East Sussex Light Railway
KLR	Kingsnorth Light Railway
L&BR	London & Brighton Railway
LBSCR	London, Brighton & South Coast Railway
LCDR	London, Chatham & Dover Railway
LSWR	London & South Western Railway
LTSR	London, Tilbury & Southend Railway
RH&DR	Romney, Hythe & Dymchurch Railway
SECR	South Eastern & Chatham Railway (the working union of the SER & LCDR from 1899)
SER	South Eastern Railway
S&KLR	Sittingbourne & Kemsley Light Railway
SVR	Spa Valley Railway
TWERPS	Tunbridge Wells & Eridge Railway Preservation Society
WVRA	Westerham Valley Railway Association

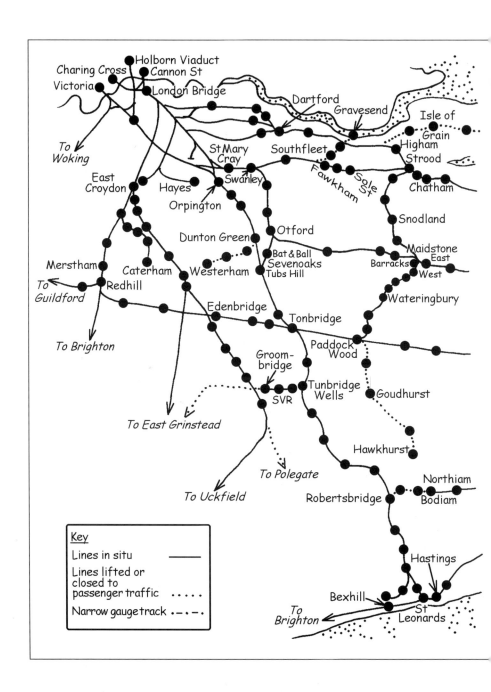

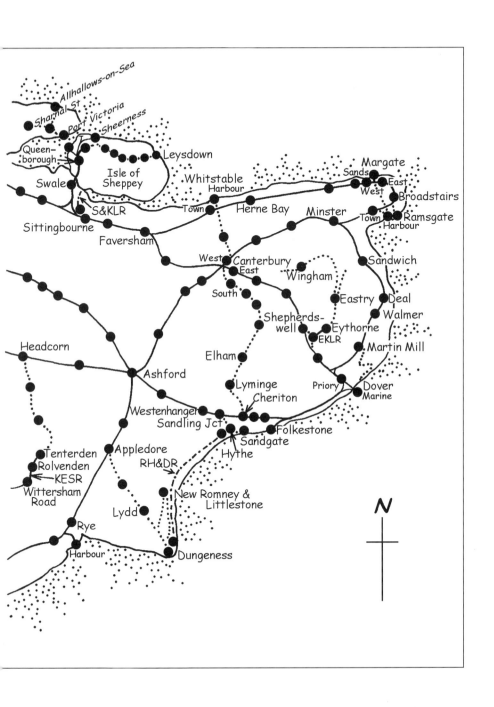

Allhallows-on-Sea
Sharnal St
Port Victoria
Sheerness
Queen-
borough
Leysdown
Swale
Isle of
Sheppey
Whitstable
Harbour
Margate
Sands
East
West
Broadstairs
S&KLR
Town
Herne Bay
Minster
Town
Ramsgate
Harbour
Sittingbourne
Faversham
West
Canterbury
East
Wingham
Sandwich
South
Eastry
Deal
Walmer
Shepherds-
well
Eythorne
EKLR
Martin Mill
Headcorn
Elham
Ashford
Lyminge
Cheriton
Priory
Dover
Marine
Westenhanger
Sandling Jct
Folkestone
Sandgate
Appledore
Hythe
Tenterden
Rolvenden
KESR
RH&DR
Wittersham
Road
New Romney &
Littlestone
Lydd
Rye
Harbour
Dungeness

N

Introduction

The standard of road transport in Kent during the 16th century was described by a Chancellor as 'ruinous beyond imagination'. Highways, frequently thick with mudded ruts, were so bad that on one occasion a traveller found it necessary to reach Horsham, in Sussex, from London via Canterbury!

With roads in such a state it was hardly surprising that commercial eyes began looking towards waterways as a means to transport their goods. In the year 1740 an Act was passed authorising the establishment of a river navigation on the Upper Medway from Maidstone to Tonbridge. Plans followed eventually to build a Grand Southern Canal from Tonbridge via Edenbridge across Sussex to Portsmouth to link Chatham with the Royal Dockyard at Portsmouth. This would avoid the hazards of the Channel during the period of the Napoleonic Wars. But the scheme, the cost of which was put at over half a million pounds, was defeated in Parliament by a large majority.

In 1806 the Royal Military Canal from Sandgate across the Romney Marshes opened, primarily intended as a defence line against possible French invasion. Eighteen years later in 1824 the first commercial canal opened, the Thames and Medway, designed to link Gravesend and Strood thus saving vessels the long haul round the Isle of Grain. The canal included a tunnel of almost 4,000 yards which was to play a part in railway history some years later.

The following year, 1825, saw two developments that were to radically affect the course of transport in the years to follow. It was the year that the Stockton & Darlington Railway opened but, as far as Kent was concerned, on 10th June that year Parliament agreed to the construction of a 'railway or tram road from the seashore at or near Whitstable, in the County of Kent, to or near the City of Canterbury in the said County'.

On 3rd May 1830 the line was formally opened. It was an event that was to coincide with the opening later the same year of the Liverpool & Manchester Railway although the Canterbury

& Whitstable Railway (CWR) never equalled the Liverpool & Manchester in importance. The CWR was, however, one of the first public railways to be built using steam traction even though stationary engines using cables to pull trains were used over steeper inclines along the line. It also claimed to include the first bridge (at Whitstable) by rail over a road. The CWR provided a useful, though perhaps not very efficient, passenger and freight service for over 100 years.

Travelling by rail was pretty uncomfortable in earlier times. Railway carriages began as stage-coach bodies attached to wagon bases. They were small, cramped and unlit and had no heating or travel facilities. Third class travel was frequently in open trucks without seats. By 1845 an Act of Parliament compelled the railway companies to provide covered coaches. Before this happened a jeweller made his name by selling special spectacles as protection against the dirt and steam.

When coach lighting came it was by oil lamps, subsequently to be replaced by gas lamps. Steam heating and comfortable seating came later that century although the 1880s saw the introduction of dining cars with kitchens, purpose-built for long distance travel. It is a sad reflection that the luxuries of Pullman car travel are today almost defunct.

By the early 1840s the development of turnpikes in the county had almost come to an end. Already there were some 50 trusts in Kent covering well over 600 miles and the last recorded to be established was from Cranbrook to Hawkhurst, today better known as the A229. Earlier in 1836 the South Eastern Railway (SER) had gained Royal Approval to build a railway across Kent from the capital to Folkestone and Dover via Oxted and Tonbridge.

In July 1837, however, the London & Brighton Railway received approval to build a line to the coast and Parliament, with remarkably little foresight, considered that one set of lines out of London was sufficient. So the SER was compelled to build a line east from Reigate Junction (known as Redhill today) to reach Ashford by the end of 1842 and Folkestone Junction by December 1843. Major developments came the following year with SER trains reaching Dover from London in February, a branch line from Maidstone Road (now Paddock Wood) to

9

Maidstone completed in September and the SER taking over the working of the Canterbury & Whitstable Railway.

Canal trade began to suffer as railways continued to spread across Kent during a period of 'railway mania'. Canterbury, Ramsgate and Margate were reached by SER trains in 1846. At the same time, the Canterbury & Whitstable Railway abandoned its earlier system of pulling trains by cables worked from stationary engines and adopted conventional locomotives throughout its length. By the following year the canal between Strood and Higham was abandoned and doubled track was laid. For a time the SER had the monopoly of railways throughout Kent but this was not to last. A company known as the East Kent Railway Company, to be known as the London, Chatham & Dover Railway Company (LCDR) from 1859, opened a line from Chatham to Faversham in January 1858. Two months later a controversial short branch from Chatham to Strood was built.

Inevitably the Turnpike Trusts came to an end around 1870 although one from Biddenden via Charing to Boundgate did go on until 1884. Certain river navigations survived a number of years but trade was not significant. The Stour River Navigation from Fordwich to Canterbury closed to commercial traffic around 1877 and sections of the Royal Military Canal lingered on until 1909.

By early last century a network of lines existed throughout the county. The majority of these have served a useful life and, of course, a large number live actively on, playing an important role. This book largely covers those lines which did not survive.

Leslie Oppitz

1
A Line To Whitstable

Sidings at Whitstable Harbour in April 1951. The Canterbury to Whitstable line closed to passengers in 1931. (John H. Meredith)

The Canterbury & Whitstable Railway was one of the first ten passenger railways in the world. It was agreed by means of an Act of 10th June 1825 and its formal opening took place on 3rd May 1830. The line was 6 miles long and throughout its early life it suffered many difficulties.

The reason for such a line was to provide Canterbury, at that time East Kent's most important market centre, with a link to the Thames Estuary. Previously the town had relied on the river Stour and its inland port, Fordwich, but silting had long been a problem and for many years alternative proposals had been considered. In 1811 a scheme was put forward to build a canal from Ashford down the Stour Valley to Canterbury and then north-eastwards to St Nicholas at Wade where it would cross to the sea. This did not happen since the railway age was dawning.

The company was initially known as the Canterbury & Whitstable Railway and construction of the line took several years of arduous digging and preparation. Work excavating the 828 yard Tyler Hill tunnel proved difficult and lengthy. By the autumn of 1826, after 15 months, only 400 yards had been completed. Work was delayed by a fall of earth but at last in May 1827 contact between the north and south ends was effected. The engineers were delighted since it meant that stale air through the tunnel could be cleared. Bearing in mind that almost 2,500 ft of track was involved, amazingly the final calculation was correct to within an inch.

The southern portal of Tyler Hill tunnel on the Canterbury to Whitstable line photographed on 21st April 1951. The line finally closed in December 1952 when freight traffic came to an end. (John H. Meredith)

The tunnel had aroused much comment and criticism. Many suggested it had been built because it had been proclaimed that 'every good railway must have a tunnel'. Nothing appears to be recorded to support this theory and a look at any Ordnance Survey map shows there was really no practical alternative.

Sections of the line were so steeply graded that stationary engines were required to haul trains by cable up the steep ascents. From Canterbury the first was at Tyler Hill with a further stationary engine at Clowes Wood to deal with trains between Tyler Hill and Bogshole Brook. The expected speed up a gradient was estimated at 9 mph. For the last 2 miles to Whitstable the locomotive *Invicta* was at first used.

There were great celebrations for the opening on 3rd May 1830. In Canterbury, the cathedral bells were rung and guns were fired in salute. There were two trains, consisting altogether of twenty carriages and twelve wagons. The whole length was bedecked with flags and the two leading carriages carried the directors, aldermen and other members of the Corporation. The third carried their ladies and the fourth, a band. A local newspaper described entering the tunnel as very impressive. It reported: 'The cheering of the whole party echoing through the vault combined to form a situation, certainly novel and striking.'

But not all the passengers enjoyed the experience. According to a letter in the local press, one traveller wrote: 'When we had proceeded halfway through, a feeling of suffocation became perceptible, increasing so fearfully that had the tunnel been twice the length, I feel confident I should have hardly got through alive.' The writer walked back to Canterbury.

As the first train reached a summit, the cable that had hauled it up the incline was transferred to some loaded wagons which, by running down again, allowed the cable to be attached to the second train. When both sections of the train had reached the final summit, the locomotive *Invicta* – delivered by sea from Newcastle – took the train to Whitstable. At Whitstable another grand ceremony followed when directors entered the harbour in a specially chartered steamer to military band accompaniment.

On the return journey the final descent down the Tyler Hill incline was made by the complete train, which was described as gliding 'rapidly and majestically into Canterbury about six o'clock'. A sumptuous dinner party followed which included a turtle weighing 1 cwt. The opening of the Canterbury & Whitstable Railway had been considered as going 'remarkably well without a single mishap'.

Unfortunately *Invicta* developed difficulties on a section of track towards Whitstable which reached 1 in 50 on one section. A third stationary engine was introduced in 1832 although for a time horses were substituted. The locomotive continued to work the lesser slopes for a while. Travelling time was beginning to suffer with some journeys taking well over an hour instead of the standard 40 minutes. This was small wonder with a single trip now comprising movement by horses, a steam locomotive, stationary steam engines and gravity.

In 1834 season tickets were introduced, the first ever in the world. A further important development came in 1836 with the formation of the Canterbury & Whitstable Steam Packet Company. A steamer (the *William the Fourth*) ran every other day between London and Whitstable with trains worked in connection.

The locomotive *Invicta* was finally withdrawn in 1839 and the whole line was cable worked until 1846. An advertisement appeared in the *Railway Magazine and Commercial Journal* of 28th September 1839 as under:

'For sale. A locomotive steam engine (taken off the Canterbury & Whitstable Railway in good repair); 12 hp. Length of stroke 18 inches; length of cylinder 2 feet; diameter 9½ inches; height of wheels 4 feet.

Apply to Mr Sanders, Whitstable. Letters post paid.'

There were no buyers so *Invicta* was stored and later a place was found for her in the Ashford works paint shop. Following numerous exhibitions, the engine was presented to the City of Canterbury in 1906 and for many years it stood in the Dane John Gardens. It can be found today at the museum in Stour Street.

Some years after regular services had begun in 1830 the original owners, the Canterbury & Whitstable Railway Company, made numerous attempts to lease the line to another operator. It was not until September 1844 that the SER took on working the line, eventually absorbing the CWR by an Act of August 1853.

14

The locomotive 'Invicta' which served on the Canterbury to Whitstable line, photographed in Canterbury in September 1948. It can currently be found in the museum in Stour Street. (John H. Meredith)

In April 1846 the SER main line from Canterbury to Ramsgate opened. Since this crossed the CWR line, the original North Lane station at Canterbury was closed to passengers and a spur built alongside the new SER station where a short bay served CWR passengers. The North Lane station remained in use for goods traffic.

It was unfortunate that Tyler Hill tunnel had been constructed with a limited bore. There were soon problems since nothing wider than 9 ft 3 ins or higher than 11 ft could pass through. After 1846, when conventional locomotives were used throughout the line, 119 class 0-6-0s were adopted and in 1883 two Stirling O class 0-6-0s had to be given cut-down chimneys. Subsequently four R class 0-6-0Ts had their boiler mountings reduced in size and these were used until closure.

During the life of the line, passenger services were infrequent and slow and the coaches, also limited by size because of the tunnel, were old and not at all comfortable. After the First World

Whitstable Harbour, 21st April 1951. Locomotive R1 0-6-0T no 31010
with a cut-down chimney to cope with the limited bore of Tyler Hill tunnel.
(John H. Meredith)

War, bus competition began to cause problems and the line to
Whitstable finally closed to passengers on 1st January 1931.
Goods traffic continued for a number of years. It was ironic that
coal, imported at Whitstable from the North of England, was
later to travel in the other direction when it became available
from Chislet Colliery in Kent. Inevitably freight closure came on
1st December 1952 after which time the track was removed.

Sections of the line can, however, still be traced. The former
goods shed at Canterbury West has been extensively refurbished
for its new role as a farmers' market. From Canterbury the track
bore sharply left from the station along the Beaconsfield Road
area and after nearly a mile entered Tyler Hill tunnel over which
the University of Kent now stands. The tunnel in fact made its
presence felt as recently as 1974 when a subsidence damaged
some of the college buildings.

Along a minor road from Tyler Hill to Blean there is a property

Canterbury West, which opened as 'Canterbury', was one of the first stations to issue season tickets. (Anthony Rispoli)

called The Halt. This private residence, converted from an engineman's cottage, was once the site of Blean and Tyler Hill Halt which was opened in 1908. Parts of the old trackbed can be walked. South from Tyler Hill Halt the original north portal of the tunnel can be found. To the north there is a track through Clowes Wood where the site of the Clowes Wood stationary engine is close by a pond and a widening of the path.

On the approach to Whitstable there are more reminders. South Street, off the A299 Thanet Way marks the site of South Street Halt (opened 1911) near a junction with Millstrood Road. A cul-de-sac off the latter is aptly named The Halt. The bridge built over Church Road which survived until 1969 claims to have been the oldest railway bridge in the world. Despite strenuous local efforts for its preservation, it was demolished because of its condition. In addition it had become too narrow

17

Whitstable Harbour station which was built in 1846, two years after the SER began working the line. The station closed to passengers in 1849 when a single-platform station was built on the other side of the road. (Lens of Sutton Collection)

A class R1 0-6-0T no A147 ex-SER at Whitstable Harbour in the late 1920s. (Lens of Sutton Collection)

for modern-day traffic. Pieces of the bridge were sold as souvenirs to raise money for charity.

The track followed between Clare Road and Station Road to cross Tower Parade to the harbour. The original Whitstable Harbour station adjacent to the Steam Packet Inn was replaced in 1846 by the South Eastern Railway (SER) soon after it had taken over the line. Sidings were built, linking to SER tracks, fanning out to both sides of the harbour. This station lasted until 1894 when it was closed and a single-platform station was built on the other side of the road. Because of this the need for a level crossing over Tower Parade was overcome.

When the last train ran on 1st January 1931, it comprised locomotive no 31010 hauling two brake vans to Whitstable with passengers, including press, radio and TV representatives. Whitstable Harbour station had been decorated for the occasion and the train was met by a crowd of about 100 people. On the return journey the train stopped at the Canterbury end of the Tyler Hill tunnel where a wreath was presented. What a proud ending for a railway that had survived just over 100 years for passengers and had become known affectionately by some as the 'Crab and Winkle' line.

2
Trains Reach Dover

Admiralty Pier at Dover, c1910. SER trains first reached the pier in 1860 and in 1864 LCDR trains reached the pier for the first time. In bad weather waves broke over the pier and trans-shipment of passengers and luggage proved very hazardous. (Lens of Sutton Collection)

An early proposal to reach Dover came in 1824 when a prospectus was issued by the Kentish Railway. The line was planned to run from London to Dover and Sandwich via Woolwich, Chatham and Canterbury (with branch lines to Maidstone and Margate). The funding required was estimated at a million pounds and the line was to be worked by 'locomotive machines' although the company would also consider 'the assistance of horses'.

In a later prospectus issued by the SER directors, a scheme of

1832 was considered. The line was to run nearly due east, much of it along the 1824 route and in parts closely following the London to Dover road. The scheme was to connect the military depots of Woolwich, Chatham, Sheerness and Dover with the capital. The idea was unusual in that the first part of the journey would commence north of the Thames across the Essex marshes. At a point opposite Woolwich it was intended that trains would cross the river on the deck of a steam ferry boat, thus avoiding for passengers the 'inconvenience of quitting their seats or removing a single article of luggage'.

Beyond Gravesend the line was planned via Upnor Castle where a further ferry would carry the train across the Medway to the north side of Chatham Dockyard. At this point a steam boat would provide a branch to Sheerness. Beyond Faversham and south of Boughton Hill to Canterbury, more branches were considered to coastal towns.

The scheme appeared highly imaginative although with minimum inconvenience to passengers. However, not only transport by rail and water was envisaged but also by road. The prospectus added that highways involved in the route would be improved since it was proposed 'to adapt the carriages that run upon it as to render them equally fit for passage over ordinary roads'. At such a point carriages would be pulled by horses although how the wheels would adapt was not disclosed. Possibly rails with inbuilt flanges were being considered – perhaps similar to tram lines that were to follow many years later.

Clearly the idea was well before its time. Local landowners objected most strongly and there was little enthusiasm from the townsfolk. The idea of crossing the Medway north of Chatham was considered a major obstacle and presumably it had not occurred to the instigators that as far as the Thames was concerned, this crossing could have been avoided by starting south of the river.

All these ideas were not to be as envisaged. In 1836 Parliament agreed a line proposed by the SER from the terminus of the London & Croydon Railway at London Bridge through Oxted, Tonbridge and Ashford to the coast. In 1837 the line from London to Brighton was sanctioned and with Parliament now

Folkestone Harbour station, c1910. The original station opened in 1849 but was resited a year later when a permanent station was completed. (Lens of Sutton Collection)

Three locomotives leave Folkestone Harbour hauling a boat train on 17th September 1949. The locomotives were ex-SECR no 31154 R11 0-6-0T, ex-SECR no 31047 R11 0-6-0T and ex-LCDR no 1708 R1 0-4-0T. (John H. Meredith)

Locomotive 3633 arrives at Folkestone Harbour with mixed freight and passenger set on 29th June 1960. (John H. Meredith)

considering that the one entrance into London from the south was enough, the SER was obliged to accept, under a section of the Act, that its line should commence at what was then Reigate Junction (now Redhill). Part of the SER route from London was to be shared with the London & Brighton Railway, a situation that later gave both companies many problems. So a line was built from Reigate Junction via Edenbridge and Tonbridge and eastwards to Dover.

SER trains reached the Kent coast from London in December 1843. The progress had been in stages over several years. Tonbridge (then called Tunbridge) commenced services on 26th May 1842. Headcorn opened three months later and Ashford was reached by the end of the same year.

The last stretch to Folkestone was completed in June 1843. Initially trains terminated at a temporary station since a viaduct was needed to cross a valley which carried a stream to the

A rather untidy terminus end at Folkestone Harbour photographed in August 2002. The station today is only rarely used. Until recently the Venice Simplon Orient Express used the station but at present nothing is scheduled. (Anthony Rispoli)

Ashford station in SER days, 12th May 1891. On the left an SER 2-4-0 locomotive of 1876. (Lens of Sutton Collection)

harbour. Foord Viaduct, which comprised 19 arches to a maximum height of over 100 ft, was completed within six months.

From Folkestone to Dover the going was tough. Progress included the digging of Martello tunnel (532 yards), Abbotscliffe tunnel (1 mile 182 yards) and Shakespeare tunnel (1,387 yards) along the coastal route. Between Abbotscliffe and Shakespeare tunnels was Round Down cliff, the summit of which was almost 400 ft high.

To overcome this obstacle a 70 ft width of chalk cliff was removed over a length of 300 ft in a sensational manner. Rather than penetrate the cliff, Engineer William Cubitt sunk three shafts and off each was a gallery, 300 ft long. At the foot of each shaft was a chamber 14 ft by 4 ft 6 ins and 5 ft high. In each of the chambers of the outer shafts he placed 5,500 lbs of gunpowder and in the middle shaft 7,500 lbs. Each charge had a battery fixed in a shed on the cliff connected with 1,000 ft of wire.

The Board of Trade was consulted and the Royal Engineers were brought in to supervise the firing. This was completed on 26th January 1843. A *Times* correspondent of the day reported that at exactly 2.26 pm 'a low, faint, indistinct, indescribable, moaning, rumbling was heard and immediately afterwards the bottom of the cliff began to belly out. Then almost simultaneously about 500 ft in breadth of the summit began gradually, but rapidly, to sink.'

The chalk was soon cleared and foundations for a track made secure. Two short sections for the railway were built along the beach. One was protected by a massive concrete sea-wall and the other by a strong timber viaduct. The latter was constructed on piles driven into the solid chalk below, yet sufficiently above high water to prevent damage by the sea. This timber bridge lasted until 1927 when it was demolished and replaced by a concrete wall.

It is hardly surprising that the stability of the chalk cliffs between Folkestone and Dover continued to cause concern over the years. In December 1915 there was a massive earth-slip at Folkestone Warren and even today the situation, particularly at Shakespeare Cliff, poses a continual threat to the main railway route. Electronic devices are set to detect any cliff movement or rock fall and such an event would automatically turn signals to

A heavy coal train hauled by Bo-Bo electric locomotive E5024 stops briefly at the east end of Shakespeare Cliff tunnel for a crew change. (Arthur Tayler)

red on the line which runs along the foot of the cliffs. It has been considered that the event of a serious cliff collapse could be so devastating that the cost of rebuilding the line would be difficult to justify.

The complete line from London to Dover opened on 7th February 1844 with the Kent terminus at what was later known as Dover Town station. At last trains reached the Channel port directly from London and the SER saw itself as providing a gateway to Europe.

The distance from London to Dover via Redhill was 87 miles (10 miles longer than the present direct route). Services were timed so that the steam packets from the French ports arrived at Dover in time for the last 'up' train. In this way passengers from France could reach London on the same day with a total journey time of about nine hours. Fares for the crossing were 6 shillings for deck passengers and 8 shillings for cabin passengers.

As was to be expected, a branch from the main Dover line soon followed to Maidstone. The line commenced at Maidstone

'Schools' class locomotive 'Hurstpierpoint' 4-4-0 no 30918 takes on water at Ashford. This is a Charing Cross to Dover train photographed in April 1950. (Arthur Tayler)

Paddock Wood station on the Tonbridge-Folkestone route, c1910. When the station opened in 1842 it was called Maidstone Road. (Lens of Sutton Collection)

Road station (renamed Paddock Wood when the branch opened) providing a single track, later doubled, over the 10 mile route, much of it following the course of the river Medway.

On the day before the official opening, trains ran all day backwards and forwards along the branch offering free rides. When services began on 25th September 1844, the line was the first to be equipped with the 'electric telegraph' system developed by the SER to give safer working.

History at Paddock Wood has almost repeated itself for just over 140 years later the control room at the station was used to 'switch on' the power for the new electrification scheme on the Tonbridge to Hastings line. On 17th March 1986 the Minister for Public Transport, Mr David Mitchell MP, made a series of changes to energise the line. He first connected the control centre with the 11,000v AC National Grid and then connected the 750v DC traction current to the conductor rails covering a service that began officially on 12th May 1986.

In July 1845 the SER had its first accident of note. It was an unusual one for when the evening train from Dover arrived at Tonbridge the last carriage was detached but its tail lights were not transferred. So after the train had left, an engine was sent with the missing lamps to catch up with it. The almost inevitable happened. It was dark when the train had stopped at Penshurst and the chasing locomotive ran into the back, injuring 30 passengers.

Six months later there was a further mishap. On the same stretch between Tonbridge and Penshurst a train was passing over a wooden bridge across a tributary of the river Medway when the supports gave way. The engine and some of the train ran into the water, killing the driver and causing much damage.

SER branch lines across Kent inevitably followed and within a few years trains reached towns such as Canterbury, Ramsgate and Tunbridge Wells. By 1851 trains reached Hastings via Robertsbridge and Battle.

Two years later Parliament gave approval to a company called the East Kent Railway (EKR) to build a line from Strood, crossing the Medway to Rochester with branches to Faversham Quay and Chilham. In addition the right to use the SER stations at Strood and Canterbury was obtained. From such modest beginnings came considerable rivalry in the years to come between two major railway companies.

But the EKR was looking southward and in 1855 powers were obtained to extend to Dover and for the first time the SER would face serious competition. By 1859 the EKR had reached Faversham from Chatham and had obtained approval to link with London to the west. The Chilham branch idea was dropped and in pressing towards the coast, no physical link was made with the Canterbury SER station. In the same year the EKR became known as the London, Chatham & Dover Railway (LCDR).

Dover Town station (now Dover Priory) was reached in July 1861 and four months later the LCDR extended to Dover Harbour. Charged with success the LCDR secured a further achievement in 1862 by obtaining the contract for carrying mail between Dover and Calais. For the previous eight years it had been held by Mr Churchward of Dover who had his own

A train emerges from Dover Priory tunnel (158 yards) to stop at Dover Priory station. A line was completed between Canterbury and Dover in 1861. (Anthony Rispoli)

Dover Marine station in the 1920s. The SECR Marine station opened in 1919 when the Admiralty Pier station was closed. (Lens of Sutton Collection)

steamers, although the mail from London to Dover had been carried by the SER. But two years later the major rail companies obtained powers to acquire and work their own boats and thereafter the mails were carried jointly.

In addition to their cross-Channel services, the LCDR also operated boats between Dover and Ramsgate calling at Deal. In 1862 an Act was passed for a railway from Dover to Deal but although this did not immediately come about, it was later constructed jointly with the SER.

With services from London and most major Kent towns now available to the Channel ports, the gateway to Europe was now considered well and truly opened.

A Wartime Recollection

Worthy of mention is a line that ran from Martin Mill to the east of Dover Harbour. Initially authorised by a Naval Works Act of 1897, a harbour extension of some 600 acres was constructed involving the building of massive breakwaters with concrete or granite blocks. Much of the gravel to make the concrete was taken from a pit at Stonar, near Sandwich, and to carry the gravel along the last stretch from Martin Mill to Dover, a contractor's rail route was provided. This branched off the main line just south of Martin Mill and, after a mile parallel to the main track, it curved away near Guston tunnel entrance to cross fields and then wound its way down the cliff to the harbour. The engineering works involved were extensive, requiring a shelf to be cut in the side of the chalk cliffs. The railway served 10 years of intensive use.

The line closed in 1909 when the harbour works had been completed. At an early stage there was talk of conversion over part of the route to a 3 ft 6 in gauge passenger line using electric traction. A Light Railway Order authorising the conversion was obtained and traffic would have come from proposed new housing estates. The scheme, however, never materialised and the original standard gauge track was taken up in 1937.

During the Second World War, part of the line was restored and this was extended to give a route resembling the letter 'U' to provide a lengthy wide-angled firing range for rail-mounted guns.

These were kept in Guston tunnel on the main line by day and brought out along the cliff route at night to bombard the French coast. Traces of the old line remain. The route down the cliff face is easy to find as also the remains of bridges, south of Hawthorn Farm Caravan and Camping Site at Martin Mill, on Hangman's Lane at Cherrytree Hole and close to *The Swinging Gate* public house where the line can clearly be traced crossing the A258.

3
Lines To Thanet

Ramsgate beach and SECR Harbour station, c1910. After closure of the station in 1926 the site became an amusement park. This was destroyed by fire in the 1990s and the area awaits future development. (Lens of Sutton Collection)

Over the years Margate has been served by as many as four different railway stations. If a planned LCDR terminus is included and another that was built but never used, the potential number increases to six.

The mid 19th century was a period of 'railway mania'. Different railway companies sought to acquire new areas before any rival concern reached the territory. Such was the case to the east of Kent where situations eventually arose giving duplicated lines and stations. Margate was a good example.

Trains first reached the Isle of Thanet in 1846 when an SER branch from Canterbury was opened to Ramsgate on 13th April. The terminus, Ramsgate Town, initially known as 'Ramsgate SER', was located towards the outskirts of the town. It had two low and short platforms with four tracks between them although later a narrow island platform was added between the two inside tracks. The terminus was situated where today Station Approach Road meets Margate Road (A254) and not far from the present station.

In order to strengthen its monopoly of the area, it was not long before the SER completed a line northwards from Ramsgate to Margate. This stretch of over 4 miles was opened in December 1846 although Margate had to be content with a temporary wooden station, Margate Sands, initially known as Margate SER, until a permanent station was built some 12 years later. The only intermediate 'station' was another wooden structure built to serve the Tivoli Pleasure Gardens, which became Tivoli Park, and close to the goods station and industrial estate.

The line from Ramsgate to Margate gave the SER a problem

Ramsgate Town station which opened in 1846 was to last 80 years. Seen here in the 1890s. (Lens of Sutton Collection)

33

since the new track branched off at the very end of the platforms. Thus a reversal was necessary and no platform enlargement was possible. To overcome this, a spur was provided in 1863 which allowed through running from Canterbury to Margate. The following year a station called St Lawrence was opened just before the spur, allowing Ramsgate passengers access to and from Margate trains but the station was closed in 1916. Despite the popularity of Margate as a seaside resort, the spur was little used.

In July 1847 a further branch was added to the SER network linking Minster (on the Canterbury to Ramsgate line) with Deal. Surprisingly it was not until 1881 that Deal was linked with Dover and then, even more surprisingly, in a joint venture between the rival LCDR and SER companies.

The SER monopoly in the Thanet area was eventually broken when the Herne Bay & Faversham Company, incorporated in

An Ashford to Ramsgate train hauled by class 24 locomotive D5002 (on loan from London Midland region) enters Minster (Thanet), January 1960. (Arthur Tayler)

Minster (Thanet) with a four-coach electric train in April 1961. The train was a new type of rolling stock on a test run from Charing Cross to Ramsgate via Canterbury. It was run at high speed over a section of track not yet opened to the public. (Arthur Tayler)

1857 against strong SER opposition, reached Herne Bay in 1861. Efforts to delay the opening were made by the SER on the grounds that the bridge under the Canterbury & Whitstable Railway was unsafe. The claim proved unjustified and the line went ahead. Further extensions eastwards were inevitable and in the same year authority was given to reach Margate. Also at that time the promoting company became known as the Kent Coast Railway.

On 5th October 1863 trains reached Margate and Ramsgate, much of the route being that used today. The LCDR worked the line from the outset and took over the smaller company in 1871. Passengers from London now enjoyed a shorter journey to the Thanet resorts, proving quicker than those circuitous routes offered by the SER.

The LCDR was quick to exploit its arrival at Margate. Initially

Locomotive 31832 awaits departure from platform 3 at Faversham station – photographed 1954. Faversham station opened in January 1858 and a branch to Canterbury was completed two years later. (Stations UK)

a terminus was planned to be sited at the top end of Station Road. Shortly before completion of the Herne Bay to Margate stretch, authority was given to extend to Ramsgate. A new station was required since the track needed to curve eastward just short of the planned station. This was built on the site of the present Margate station and at first was a small two platform affair known as 'Margate C&D'.

Beyond where the new LCDR track crossed the line from 'Margate SER', a further station was built as a terminus on a spur and adjoining the SER station. But it was never used and it was let to a firm of caterers who called it 'Hall by the Sea'. Later it became part of Dreamland Amusement Park when all railway traces were lost.

Yet another LCDR station was soon to be opened, inland from the coast, and called Margate East. This was situated to the east of the bridge where Ramsgate Road (A254) crosses the track today. The station opened in 1870 and closed in 1953.

After a long straight run and then a curve into Broadstairs, the

LCDR route of 1863 reached Ramsgate. Here the LCDR had considerable advantage over the SER inland station since their terminus was built along the seafront itself. To achieve this, trains were required to descend a 1 in 75 cutting and then a 1,630 yard tunnel to come out into the platforms of 'Ramsgate C&D', directly adjacent to the beach and very close to the harbour. This station comprised two long platforms with numerous tracks and the building was partly covered.

In 1899 the LCDR and SER amalgamated to become the South Eastern & Chatham Railway (SECR) and further complicated changes followed. 'Margate C&D' became Margate West, the earlier SER station became Margate Sands and, for no obvious reason, East Margate was changed to Margate East. At the southern end, 'Ramsgate SER' became Ramsgate Town and 'Ramsgate C&D' was called Ramsgate Harbour.

The anomalies over duplicated services remained and it was not until 1926 that any radical changes were made. The SECR had planned alterations but they were never carried out so it

Margate Sands station photographed around 1914. Loco no 1067 is from the GNR and loaned to the SECR to ease an engine shortage. (Lens of Sutton Collection)

became the responsibility of the Southern Railway, formed with grouping in 1923. On 2nd July 1926 a new line almost 1½ miles long was opened from the vicinity of Ramsgate Town to a point on the LCDR line near Dumpton Park where a new station of that name was opened. This created a new through station at Ramsgate while the old Ramsgate Town station was closed down. Inevitably the old 1846 SER route across the peninsula became redundant and in addition the line down to the harbour terminus was abandoned. No doubt this latter decision was not well received by the passengers since the new station at Ramsgate was as remotely situated as the previous Ramsgate Town.

The triangular area at the old Ramsgate Town station disappeared and its place was taken by new locomotive and carriage depots. The new Ramsgate station was built with rather a dramatic frontage, perhaps to boost its importance after

Ramsgate station, August 2002. The original Ramsgate Town station closed in 1926 to be renamed Ramsgate and resited at its present location. (Anthony Rispoli)

closure of the harbour station. Margate was rebuilt in the same style.

Thus the pattern was set for the Thanet lines as they are known today. The area now simply incorporates a circular route with many trains arriving daily from London via Chatham and also via Ashford and Dover. But what is left from the past?

The SER 1846 line from Ramsgate Town to Margate Sands closed in July 1926. Ramsgate Town station was lost to development but for many years a retaining wall from the old station remained evident in the Chatham Street area. Northwards, after passing property boundaries between Whitehall Road and Alkeley Road, the route is lost through the Westwood Industrial Estate. Towards Margate, part of the old track passed through what became Margate goods station. Near a bridge close to College Road there was once an SER railwayman's cottage which in later years was converted to, of all things, a public convenience!

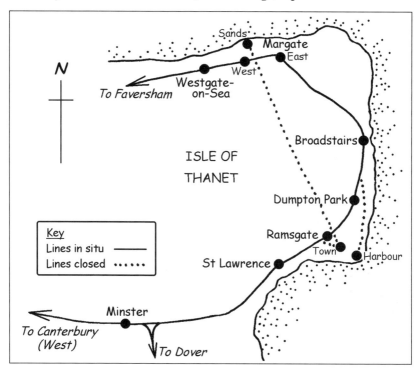

Margate Sands station became a casino bar utilising the old station frontage in the late 1950s but it is now a block of flats.

When Ramsgate Harbour station closed, the site was purchased by Thanet Amusements Ltd, which provided a fun fair, refreshment facilities and a small zoo using parts of the old station building. The opportunity of the abandoned tunnel seemed too good to miss and eventually part of it was used for an electric railway terminating at Hereson Road not far from Dumpton Park station. By this means it was hoped to not only provide transport from Dumpton Park to the seafront but also attract pleasure-riders. For the latter, about ¼ mile of the old tunnel was used to erect illuminated tableaux beside the 2 ft gauge single track. To complete the new railway, a further section of about 260 yards had to be excavated to reach the Hereson Road terminal.

The electric railway opened on August Bank Holiday 1936 with two trains, each consisting of four cars with the end one motored. For four years the line was open for the summer seasons but it was closed for six years from 1939 when the tunnel was used as an air-raid shelter during the war. From 1946 the railway survived for nearly 20 years, finally closing on Sunday, 26th September 1965.

For many years the old Ramsgate Harbour station remained an amusement park but in the late 1990s application was made for the site to become a superstore. At the same time, the amusement park suffered an unexplained disastrous fire. At the time of writing this book the site's future remains undecided. Both entrances to the tunnel used by the narrow gauge electric trains can still be found but they are sealed off. Ramsgate's railway station of today is over a mile from the harbour and beach but, in these days of motorcars, nobody seems to worry.

4
A Horse Tramway And
A Line To Sandgate

Four-wheeled 'birdcage' stock at Sandgate station, 1891.
(Lens of Sutton Collection)

In 1803 there was a serious fear that invasion from France was imminent so a canal was dug, some 30 miles in length, solely for defence purposes. Known as the Royal Military Canal, it was constructed from Shorncliffe Camp near Sandgate passing westwards through Hythe and then skirting Romney Marsh to Cliff End, near Hastings. It was close to the Sandgate end of this canal that a railway terminus was opened just over 70 years later in 1874. In 1892 a tramway system followed, close to its southern bank along Princes Road.

The SER branch line from the main line at Sandling Junction to Sandgate via Hythe was approved by Parliament in 1864. The basic idea was to serve Shorncliffe Camp by giving access to the main line from Folkestone to Ashford. Another plan was to develop Seabrook, just a mile west of Sandgate, as a holiday resort and it was here that Sandgate station was planned.

Construction of the line was delayed by a financial crisis within the railway company in 1866 and it was not until 1874 that the branch was completed. At this stage the SER revealed plans to extend the line to Folkestone Harbour, hoping to provide a better approach to the harbour facilities. A continuation of the line from Sandgate along the top of the beach was proposed to give a greatly improved access instead of the existing awkward junction and steep gradient.

The idea did not appeal to the people of Folkestone despite the fact that the SER Chairman, Sir Edward Watkin, visited the area to address a public meeting. In addition the plan was opposed by Lord Radnor with the result that the line was authorised to approach Folkestone by means of a tunnel. No doubt recalling their problems in 1843 when sections of chalk cliff had to be blasted out to provide a trackbed, the railway authorities never went ahead with such an expensive venture and Sandgate station remained the terminus.

Initially branch trains had to make their connections with the main line at Westenhanger, but 14 years later in 1888 this situation improved when a station at Sandling Junction was opened at a point where the tracks met. This proved a far more suitable arrangement with separate platforms for the branch.

Over the years the traffic using the line was only moderate, particularly since Hythe and Sandgate stations were inconveniently sited above the towns they served. In an attempt to overcome this, the SER became involved in a horse tramway system to link the stations with the busier areas.

Many Acts were submitted and either approved or rejected before a final proposal was carried out. At one stage tramlines of 3 ft 6 in gauge were proposed and at another a steam locomotive was purchased from the Sudan to work the lines. Neither idea was adopted. Finally standard gauge was agreed with horse traction only to be used.

Standard gauge had its advantages since part of a railway siding that ran along Princes Parade was incorporated as tram track. Another track section ran up Cannongate Road to Hythe

From May 1891 a standard-gauge horse tramway existed between Hythe and Sandgate, seen here along the seafront, c1918. The service came to an end in 1921. (Pamlin Prints)

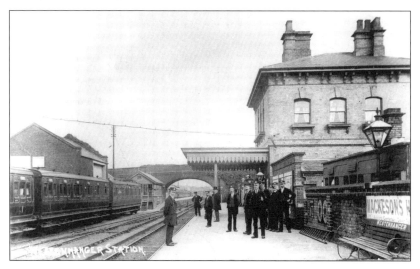

Westenhanger station, c1905. From 1874 to 1888 trains from Sandgate and Hythe made their main lines connections here. (Lens of Sutton Collection)

Sandling Junction – pre First World War. A class D 4-4-0 and passenger set leave for Ashford with a Sandgate branch train in the background. (Lens of Sutton Collection)

station but, despite the initial intentions of the SER in its involvement, this was hardly used for passenger traffic and later became derelict. The first tramline to be completed ran from Sandgate School to the Seabrook Hotel (later the Imperial Hotel) via Sandgate High Street, the Esplanade, the Promenade and Princes Parade. The section opened in May 1891 with the service operated by the Folkestone, Sandgate & Hythe Tramways Company.

Construction towards Hythe continued via South Road, Stade Street and Rampart Road, terminating in Red Lion Square, and this opened in June 1892. The section involved many sharp curves and cars were equipped with water tanks on the platforms with taps which could be turned on to lubricate the wheels when bends were negotiated.

In 1893 the SER was authorised by Parliament to take over the tramway completely, at a cost of nearly £27,000. When the transaction had been completed staff were fitted out with railway guard type uniforms. At Sandgate at least, there was a physical connection between tram and train lines and this was put to good advantage when any of the five tram cars available needed overhaul. The car was transferred to the railway and taken to Ashford Works for the necessary work. Earlier in 1892 this rail connection had been used to transport materials used in the construction of Sandgate Hill funicular railway.

Unlike many contemporary systems, the Hythe to Sandgate tramway remained horse-drawn throughout its life. In 1905 a company with well advanced plans for electric tramways in Folkestone (which never materialised) proposed to take over the Hythe to Sandgate line and electrify it. The idea was thrown out by the local authorities who opposed the use of overhead wires. In 1906 the British Electric Traction Co suggested that large sums for road works could be made available if a scheme was granted from Folkestone to New Romney. Sandgate Urban District Council liked the idea and gave notice to the railway company (SECR from 1899) that it would acquire the section of horse tramway in its boundaries for this purpose but the intention was never followed through.

When the war came in 1914 trains from Sandling Junction to Sandgate continued to provide a service but the trams were suspended due to the shortage of horses which were needed in France. Trams restarted in 1919 but horses were still difficult to find so ex-army mules were tried instead. The result apparently was catastrophic. The mules were erratic and not only stopped in the wrong places but often tried to walk in the wrong direction or into the wrong street. Horses were reinstated as soon as possible.

Already the tram service was beginning to lose its appeal. Uniforms were no longer provided and there were no winter services. When trams stopped for the season on 30th September 1921 it was to be for the last time. However, matters did not rest there. The council wrote to the SECR saying that the track would be replaced with Kentish ragstone at the railway's expense. The railway reacted by stating they wished to exercise their option under the Tramways Act by taking over the tramway in their territory and working it themselves. The council was not interested and told the railway company that any reinstatement would render them liable for costs plus surveyor's fees. This appeared to end the matter.

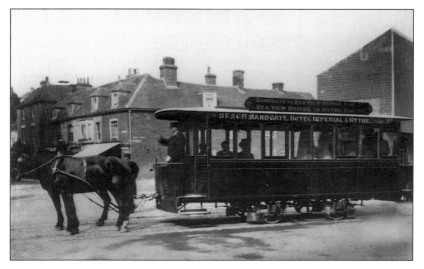

An SECR horse tram between Hythe and Sandgate, c1905. In 1919 ex-army mules were used but journeys were sometimes erratic with wrong stops and attempts to walk in different directions! (Picture courtesy Kent Education and Libraries)

In 1927 there was an interesting development from the newly-constructed narrow gauge Romney, Hythe & Dymchurch Railway (RH&DR). Consideration was given to an extension from the Hythe terminal to Sandling Junction on the main line. However, it was decided that funds could best be spent by extending the RH&DR from New Romney to Greatstone and then across the pebbles to Dungeness.

Traffic on the branch line remained light since users were finding it more convenient to patronise the main line stations. It was no surprise therefore when the section from Hythe to Sandgate closed completely and between Sandling Junction and Hythe the track became single. The site of Sandgate station was used to build a garage for the East Kent Road Car Company and all that remained of the station building was the gentlemen's toilet reserved for the bus crews. In the late 1980s when the garage was demolished to make way for flats, old railway lines were discovered some 3 ft below the ground. In addition many boulders were found, brought down from higher ground, since the area had been subjected to a serious landslip well over 100 years ago.

During the Second World War the line to Hythe closed down in 1943 only to reopen in 1945 with two trains a day. Clearly the branch was uneconomical for the Southern Railway who had no intention of encouraging traffic and it was perhaps unexpected that the line lasted another six years. The last train ran on 3rd December 1951 and Sandling Junction was renamed Sandling. At Hythe a Union Jack was flown at half-mast from the parapet of the station bridge underneath which was hung a laurel wreath and a notice reading 'R.I.P.'.

For many years all that remained at the main line end was a rusting siding along the branch platform. The track has since been removed but the platform edging remains. Hythe station stood just below the junction of Cannongate Road and Cliff Road, an area which has now been developed.

In early 1987 the RH&DR announced it was considering the idea once again to build a 4 mile link between Hythe and Sandling stations. With the Hythe branch having been closed to

Hythe station, c1932, looking towards Sandgate. The last train through the station ran in December 1951. The area today is totally redeveloped. (Stations UK)

Sandling Junction became just Sandling after closure of the branch line to Hythe in 1951. The bay platform survives today but it no longer serves trains. The footway on the right is an access ramp for disabled people. (Anthony Rispoli)

passenger trains over the route since 1951, the RH&DR thought the link could have a considerable potential. It was added that before serious thought could be given to the project, the problem of severe gradients and possibly a tunnel would have to be borne in mind.

It is already more than 80 years since the horse tram days and over 50 years since the Hythe branch closed completely. Unhappily it was a branch line that never really succeeded.

5
The Isle Of Sheppey And A Narrow Gauge Railway

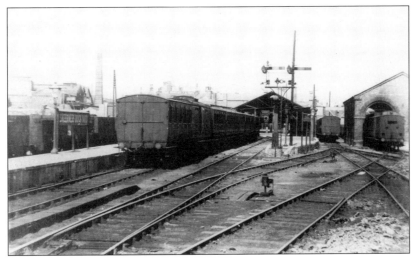

Sheerness Dockyard (opened in 1860 as Sheerness) station closed to passenger trains in 1922 and to freight in 1963. After goods closure the engine shed was used by Sheerness Steel. (Lens of Sutton Collection)

The LCDR line from Sittingbourne to Sheerness on Sea opened in July 1860. The terminus was initially Sheerness but this was changed to Sheerness Dockyard when the town's present station opened in June 1883. From this date, trains called at both stations with the need to reverse but when a spur was opened in 1922 trains were able to bypass the dockyard station which was duly closed to passenger traffic. For many years all that remained of the latter was an old engine shed used by Sheerness Steel.

Sheerness developed as a busy port and the area became dependent on rail transport. The line was electrified in 1959 and

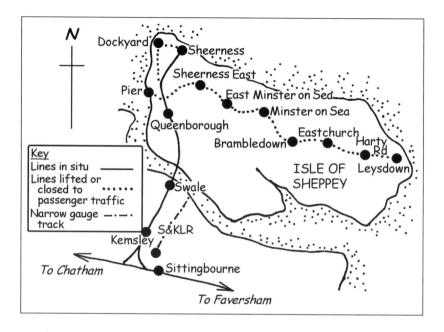

doubled from Sittingbourne to Swale Halt just short of Kingsferry Bridge.

A short branch line from Queenborough, an intermediate station on the line to Sheerness, opened in May 1876 to reach Queenborough Pier. This was built following an agreement with the Zealand Shipping Company to transfer the Ramsgate terminal of its Flushing (now known as Vlissingen) service to Sheerness. This obviously did not please the rival SER who responded with the opening of Port Victoria in 1882.

Queenborough Pier had a disastrous fire in 1882 and for a time the Flushing service was transferred to Dover. The pier was rebuilt but in 1897 floods on the Sheerness branch stopped the service once again.

There was a second disastrous fire in 1900 when the pier was destroyed once again and the LCDR now suffered the anguish of seeing their much-prized boat service transferred for some months to the SER Port Victoria terminal across the river.

Queenborough Pier closed in November 1914 and, after the Second World War, Flushing steamers were reinstated at

Queenborough Pier on the Isle of Sheppey early last century rebuilt after its second disastrous fire. (Lens of Sutton Collection)

Parkeston Quay. There was a brief reopening in 1923 after Kingsferry Bridge was damaged. The branch line remained open in theory for goods traffic although it was hardly used. In 1939 the Admiralty took over the site.

When the Second World War ended the branch lingered on until 1956 by which time the pier had been demolished. Much of the track was taken up following development of the area and today Pier Road off Whiteway Road serves only as a reminder of the past.

The Sheppey Light Railway from Queenborough to Leysdown was very much a speculative line built in the hope that Leysdown would become a popular seaside resort and residential centre.

In the draft proposal presented to the Light Railway Commissioners a maximum speed of 35 mph was suggested with a 10 mph limit over ungated level crossings. Capital was fixed at £60,000 with powers for the LCDR to subscribe and a clause requesting the ability to borrow an additional £20,000 if required. Maximum fares were proposed at 3d a mile first class, 2d for second class and 1d for third class. Due to the existing sparseness of the locality, certain stopping places would not require platforms so the lowest step on the coaches was not to be more than 16 inches above the ground.

At an enquiry held at the Town Hall in Queenborough in April 1898, the promoters agreed to divert northwards the original line planned, bringing trains closer to Sheerness and Minster. It was considered this would benefit local agriculture which was already suffering from imported food. The possibility of a railway hotel at Leysdown was also considered but this was not recommended.

Members of the Sheerness Chamber of Commerce felt the northwards diversion was not enough and they requested that the northern end of the line should commence from Sheerness instead of Queenborough. Not only would this benefit the town but it would also be useful for passengers using the SER route via Port Victoria who crossed to Sheerness by ferry. The Commission pointed out that this defeated the idea of making Leysdown accessible to London and the idea was rejected. The Chamber's request was, however, partly met by construction of a tramway in 1903 linking Sheerness East railway station with Sheerness Dockyard station.

The Sheppey Light Railway was authorised by a Light Railway Order on 3rd May 1899. The engineer appointed to supervise construction of the line was Colonel H.F. Stephens, already well known for his work on the Hawkhurst branch line and many others. In his report Colonel Stephens said that only one person objected to the line, a farmer, Mr Goodwin, tenant of Harp's Farm. Mr Goodwin complained that the railway would run across his land but promises of compensation and an occupational crossing satisfied him.

The Commissioners agreed in favour of the railway going ahead but restricted the maximum speed of the Light Railway to 25 mph. The promoters argued this point and the resultant negotiations took many months. The Order was finally approved over a year later but the speed limit remained at 25 mph. The contract to build the line was awarded to Mr W. Rigby and the first train reached Leysdown on 1st August 1901.

Construction had not been difficult as this was a surface line throughout with no earthworks. Although the highest point was only 100 ft above sea level, gradients were surprisingly steep with inclines of 1 in 70 and 1 in 80 and the line was described as 'resembling a deflated switchback'. There were no bridges but a number of level crossings, eight being on public roads. Stations, with buildings of corrugated iron in true Colonel Stephens style, were provided at Sheerness East, Minster on Sea, Eastchurch and Leysdown.

With the prospect of a new estate near Minster, a station was opened in 1902 about half a mile to the west of Minster on Sea station and called East Minster on Sea. This geographical anomaly possibly arose over the need to avoid confusing the station with 'Westminster'! With the intention of promoting traffic from agriculture, sidings had been built at Brambledown between Minster and Eastchurch and at Harty Road between Eastchurch and the terminus. These two locations became halts in 1905.

Traffic was sparse throughout the life of the line which was operated from its opening by the SECR which took it over in 1905. At this time Wainwright designed his first two steam railcars and these were used on the Sheppey Light Railway for seven years. For freight duties and for rail motorcar relief, a 'Terrier' 0-6-0 tank engine was purchased from the LBSCR. This was no 654 formerly *Waddon* built at Brighton in 1875 and bought for £670. The locomotive was renumbered 751 by the SECR and it was known locally as *Little Tich*, named after a music hall comedian who came from Kent.

Little Tich lasted five years when it was replaced by a new SECR tank locomotive, no 27. In 1912 the railcars were withdrawn although the carriage portions with the locomotive part removed went on to serve the line for almost 50 years. During this time much of the freight business was lost to road transport but this was partly offset by traffic serving an RAF station south of Eastchurch where a private siding had been built. This area had been a military flying establishment dating back to before the First World War, although after the last war the site became an open prison.

On 26th April 1935 there was a collision between a private car and a train at an ungated crossing at Minster. The incident seems hardly surprising when it is considered that of the seven stations

The branch line from Queenborough to Leysdown closed in December 1950. A class R1 0-4-4 tank locomotive plus articulated coach set on push-pull duties in Southern Railway days. (Lens of Sutton Collection)

An ex-SECR railmotor with articulated unit 513 at Queenborough on the Sheppey Light Railway, February 1948. (John H. Meredith)

along the single track branch, three were unmanned and four staffed only by a single porter. On the day in question the porter at Minster had gone off duty.

Despite the hopes of the railway authorities, Minster and Leysdown failed to provide adequate passenger traffic. An earlier idea to build a 7,000 ft long pier at Minster to attract steamers between London and Margate at all tides never materialised. An hotel for 1,200 guests at Leysdown was similarly abandoned. In 1938, railway officials visited Leysdown to consider setting up a holiday camp. Although some camps eventually materialised, it was too late. Holidaymakers were arriving in cars or on motorcycle combinations and this was no help to the ailing railway. It was clear an end was in sight although this did not come about until 1950.

The last train, an R1 class 0-4-4 engine, no 31705, plus articulated set no 514, left Queenborough for Leysdown at 4.27 pm on Saturday, 2nd December 1950 with the locals turning out in force to give the line a grand farewell. At Leysdown there was a solemn

Locomotive R1667 runs round a passenger set at Leysdown station on the Isle of Sheppey, 14th February 1948. The station closed in 1950. (John H. Meredith)

procession from the town to the station when four 'mourners' bore a mock coffin draped in black and bearing the inscription: 'In memory of the Sheppey Light that died through lack of puff'.

Today little of the branch line exists. Leysdown station area is now a car and coach park while at Sheerness East the concrete-faced platform survived many years. Otherwise alignments of trees and hedgerows are all that remain of this branch line which lasted just under half a century.

The Sittingbourne & Kemsley Light Railway

It would be a pity whilst in the area not to visit a most unusual narrow gauge railway. Unusual because when it was built numerous streets had to be crossed, so a section of the 2 ft 6 in gauge track had to be carried by a half-mile viaduct of reinforced concrete.

Well known today as the Sittingbourne & Kemsley Light Railway, it can be located in a lane off Milton Road and not far from the Sittingbourne BR station. Its origins go back to well before the First World War when wood pulp and coal for mills, located on the Medway and the Swale, were imported by steamers then unloaded into barges at various points.

In the case of Edward Lloyd's mill (subsequently Bowaters), the barges brought their cargoes to a wharf at Milton Creek where a short section of railway, opened in 1906, completed the journey. But the owners of Edward Lloyd's mill pondered a way to eliminate the time-consuming barge link and proposed that the railway should be extended to reach the incoming steamers. Two docks were built which could accommodate sea-going vessels.

Ridham Dock on the Swale was almost completed by 1913 but there were delays during the First World War. The Admiralty established a salvage depot at the site with a standard gauge railway connection to the Sheerness branch line. In 1919 Ridham Dock passed back to its owners and by this time an extension of the narrow gauge railway had been built to their Sittingbourne

56

Sittingbourne & Kemsley Railway locomotives 'Alpha' and 'Conqueror' photographed at Ridham (Bowaters) in June 1967. (R.K. Blencowe)

Brazil class 0-4-2ST locomotive 'Premier' (built 1905) hauls a passenger train on the preserved Sittingbourne & Kemsley Light Railway. The engine is currently waiting an overhaul. (Photograph courtesy and copyright Sittingbourne & Kemsley Light Railway Limited)

works. A second wharf was completed bringing coal closer to the works via Grovenhurst Dock.

The scheme proved successful and in 1924 a second works was built at Kemsley – halfway between Ridham Dock and Sittingbourne. The single track narrow gauge line between Kemsley and the dock was doubled and additional steam locomotives were purchased. The new Kemsley works was located in an isolated position on the marshes and railway traffic extended when a regular service of workmen's trains was provided which lasted until as recently as 1968.

In addition to the narrow gauge system, a standard gauge siding from the Sheerness branch line was extended to serve both Ridham Dock and Kemsley Mill. From Ridham Dock to Kemsley a substantial overhead ropeway system to carry raw materials was used and the trains underneath were protected from falling logs by a great net.

In 1969 Bowaters decided the railway was no longer the most economic means to meet their transport requirements. However, the company felt an attachment to the system that had served them so reliably, so a suitable society was sought to take over the stretch of line from Sittingbourne to Kemsley since this could be conveniently severed from the rest of their transport system.

On 4th October 1969 the section was formally handed over to the Locomotive Club of Great Britain at a special ceremony and two years later the lease passed to the Sittingbourne & Kemsley Light Railway Ltd. Today regular services for passengers operate most weekends from April to October with extra services at holidays. Here visitors can truly relive the past by seeing two of the engines, *Premier* and *Leader* both 0-4-0ST, that date back to 1906 when the first section of the line began.

6
A Branch Line To Westerham

Westerham station, c1905. The line closed in 1961 after 80 years service.
(Lens of Sutton Collection)

On 6th July 1881 the streets of Westerham were gaily decorated, the King's Arms Hotel was covered with bunting and the front of the Town Hall was festooned with flags. It was a day to remember. At the town entrance there was a triumphal arch of evergreen and colour carrying the words 'Success to the Railway' and on the other side 'Onward', the motto of the South Eastern Railway.

This was the long awaited day when trains reached Westerham from the main line at Dunton Green. Travelling was free for the day. The first 'special' left Westerham for Brasted and Dunton Green and back again bearing dozens of excited school children with their teachers, and further trains during the afternoon carried the general public.

At 4.10 pm a special train left Charing Cross for Westerham carrying the Chairman, General Manager and Directors of the railway company. They were met at the terminus by the Tunbridge Wells Parade Band who accompanied them to the Town Hall for a grand banquet. The day finished with a splendid firework display on Westerham Common, this time accompanied by the Westerham New Town Band.

The railway had not been easily obtained. The town had needed a rail link for many years and although the SER had been granted powers to construct on three previous occasions, nothing further had been done. Finally several local wealthy people promoted a Bill in 1876 having become frustrated with the SER failures.

The proposal was two-fold. Firstly a line from Dunton Green to Westerham and then a second line from Westerham to Oxted where it would join the Croydon and Oxted line (at that time not completed). This upset the SER who wanted no involvement with the Oxted line, foreseeing trouble with the LBSCR. Accordingly when the Westerham Valley Railway promoters put their plan to the House of Commons on 22nd March 1876, the first plan was adopted but the idea of a line to Oxted was rejected. At the same time it was stipulated that the SER should provide plant and rolling stock and undertake to work the line at 50% of gross receipts.

Despite these agreements nothing further happened for three years. It was inevitable that the SER should eventually take over the independent company and this happened under an agreement dated 25th June 1879 when the SER undertook to build the line. Not surprisingly, the Chairman of the SER was also a Director of the Westerham Valley Railway Company.

Work began in October 1879 over the 5 mile route. Most of the track was to be on a fairly straight and level course and it was to be single throughout. The project was completed almost two years later despite very hot weather and at a total cost of some £70,000.

The line ran along part of the Vale of Holmesdale below the North Downs through very pretty countryside. At Dunton

Green, just north of Sevenoaks, the branch connected alongside the main line with a separate platform and a run-round loop. One and a quarter miles from Dunton Green was Chevening Halt (not opened until 16th April 1906) with its short unmanned concrete platform. Brasted station was almost 2 miles further on with a single platform and small goods yard. Similarly Westerham had a single platform with a single-storey timber building and goods yard, typical of many in the SER.

When services began there were eleven 'up' and 'down' trains on weekdays and eight each way on Sundays (reduced to five within four months). Cooperation with the main line at Dunton Green was poor. The SER had no intention of stopping its fast trains to connect, so Westerham line travellers had to change to stopping trains up to London. Indeed, a few branch trains had no connection with London trains at all.

By the 1890s, trains were hauled by Cudworth 118 class 2-4-0 locomotives dating from 1859. Carriages were probably four-wheelers since at that time even the main line trains were mostly nothing better than six-wheeled carriages. Soon Stirling Q class 0-4-4 tank locomotives were to take over from the Cudworths proving themselves useful for suburban work. When the SER amalgamated with its old rival the LCDR in August 1899 to become the SECR, coaches improved and by 1900 there was even a through train – the 8.40 am from Westerham to Cannon Street. In 1906, as an economy measure, two railmotors built by Kitson of Leeds were introduced to the branch. These did not prove very efficient and, with the amount of traffic underestimated, small Wainwright engines P class 0-6-OT were introduced. They were not very powerful but for a time coped adequately on the Westerham line. They were popular tank engines and a number still exist today on preserved lines. At about the same time there were improvements to services with two through workings each morning to Cannon Street incorporating ordinary carriage stock.

In 1915 the SECR produced ambitious proposals to electrify the line from Charing Cross and Victoria to Orpington. A second stage included Orpington to Tonbridge and the Westerham branch. A 1,500v DC system was planned with current fed into two conductor rails. The idea never materialised and it was not until 1925 that the Orpington line was electrified from Holborn

Viaduct (via Nunhead) and another ten years before Sevenoaks (Tubs Hill) was reached. This was in the days of the Southern Railway which adopted the 600v DC third rail system widely used today. Westerham never saw electric trains although perhaps if it had, its untimely demise might have been quite different.

In the early Southern Railway days the coaches were ex-LCDR, six-wheeled vehicles, push-pull fitted. In an interesting and comprehensive booklet entitled *Westerham Valley Railway*, David Gould has written that the third class coaches included a spittoon at each corner of the compartments, comprising a hunk of cloth screwed to the floor!

In 1936 the Southern Railway experimented with a Sentinel-Cammell Rail Bus but it was not very successful. It was originally built for use on the Devil's Dyke branch in Sussex. Being high-geared, it was considered suitable to keep up with the electric trains on the coastal route from Brighton. The gradient up the Dyke had proved too much and, coming down again, its brakes were inadequate. The Westerham branch seemed ideal and straightaway the local journey time was reduced from thirteen to ten minutes. The car had capacity for 44 passengers but had no first class. Unfortunately, it soon became unreliable and broke down fairly frequently and by the end of the year it was taken off.

The Westerham line continued without major incident during the Second World War. Stations and trains were 'blacked out' and some services withdrawn. Perhaps the only happening of note was immediately before the war when a brick wrapped in a handkerchief was thrown through the booking office window at Brasted station. All the thief got for his trouble was two tickets and a pair of pliers.

By 1952 Dunton Green saw 22 departures on weekdays, 20 on Saturdays and 15 on Sundays. Although off-peak traffic had become light, there were up to 100 commuters during the week. However, this was a time when steam was being eliminated and the provision of rolling stock for the Westerham line was expected to prove difficult. By April 1960 closure notices were posted although at first nobody realised the furore that was to follow.

British Rail claimed the branch was losing money although

A class H 0-4-4T 31308 push-pull train at Westerham in the early 1950s. (Lens of Sutton Collection)

A motor-train approaches Chevening Halt on the Westerham branch line not long before closure of the line in 1961. (John H. Meredith)

Two ex-SECR class H tank locos with two coaches at Dunton Green on the Westerham branch line, c1952. (Lens of Sutton Collection)

little attempt had been made to investigate economies. The closure was delayed initially since the Central Transport Users' Consultative Committee recommended the line stay open as a social need. However, in August 1961 Mr Ernest Marples, the Minister of Transport, shocked the local populace by rejecting the Committee's recommendation to keep trains working with the result that official closure was announced. The last train was to run in October 1961.

The local community was incensed. Nearly 2,500 people signed a petition and hundreds wrote to their local MP. When Mr Marples was challenged in the House of Commons, he claimed that the train service was losing £26,000 per annum – over £150 for each regular passenger. He said he had given the closure very careful consideration – even to walking the area wearing dark glasses so he would not be recognised. Closure would go ahead, he said, and the date was set for Saturday, 28th October 1961. It was later suggested that the reason for closure was connected with the proposed construction of a South Orbital Road (now known as the M25) but Mr Marples claimed that 'such an idea was unfounded'.

On the last day, the engine was adorned with a Union Jack and the inscription 'Flyer 1881–1961' was chalked on the smoke box. Vast crowds arrived to 'celebrate' the occasion. When the final train, the 7.50 pm Dunton Green to Westerham, reached the terminus, the area was swamped with visitors. It was a six-coach train hauled by Q1 class 0-6-0 no 33029. One of the passengers was Mrs Jane Graves who had been a passenger on the first train in 1881.

It was inevitable that a society should consider reopening the line on an independent basis. In March 1962 the newly-formed Westerham Valley Railway Association (WVRA) met to discuss the options available. BR had agreed to sell the line for £30,000 on condition a commuter service was run since BR was subsidising bus services to replace their trains at a cost of £8,700 a year. The committee felt a service would be possible by using railcars.

In July 1962 the WVRA obtained a lease on Westerham station building which became its headquarters. Membership of the Association was encouraged and much voluntary work was carried out. The SECR colour scheme was adopted when repainting the station building. Purchase of three ex-GWR diesel railcars at £600 each was considered, plus two H class 0-4-4Ts, nos 31518 and 31263, inspected at Three Bridges and found to be in good condition. These were priced at £1,000 each.

At this stage, Kent County Council stepped in threatening compulsory purchase of the line, anxious to convert part of the track to become a section of the long-promised M25 motorway. Because of the Council's action, BR were forced to break off negotiations with the WVRA. Kent County Council finally won the day by stating that the WVRA could keep their line if they paid £26,215 for a bridge to carry the M25 over the track at Chevening (earlier estimated at £14,000!). The sum had to be paid in full otherwise the cutting at Chevening would be immediately filled in, a condition they knew the Association could not meet.

Through these over-riding actions, the Westerham Valley branch line finally died. By autumn 1964 part of the trackbed had been destroyed and locomotives and stock purchased had to be found other homes. Commuters were left to the mercy of the local bus services.

Today at Dunton Green station the site of the branch platform

Passengers await a train at Brasted on the Westerham Valley branch line. The site is now part of the M25 motorway. (Lens of Sutton Collection)

can be clearly determined in an area where a subway passes underneath. To the west of Chevening the M25 motorway covers much of the original trackbed. Brasted station has completely gone as has the terminus at Westerham. The location of the latter was to the north of the town opposite the Crown Inn, just off the A233 road from Westerham to Biggin Hill. The station site has been completely lost to industrial development although to the east, sections of trackbed can still be identified. The days of the 'Westerham Flyer' are truly over.

7
Rival Companies Meet At Tunbridge Wells

*East Grinstead to Tunbridge Wells
Spa Valley Railway*

East Grinstead to Tunbridge Wells

D3 class locomotive 0-4-4T no 2386 awaits departure from Tunbridge Wells West bound for Eastbourne on 22nd May 1948. (John H. Meredith)

A day out in Tunbridge Wells can prove very rewarding. The town is well known for its famous Pantiles, a long Georgian shopping arcade with an opportunity to 'take the water' during the summer months. There is an exhibition 'A Day at the Wells' within the Pantiles described as an exhibition 'for all the senses'. A few minutes away is the Central station with connections to London and the South Coast at Hastings.

Yet there was a time when Tunbridge Wells had two railway stations. One was Tunbridge Wells West opened by the London, Brighton & South Coast Railway (LBSCR) on 1st October 1866 and closed in 1985. The other was Tunbridge Wells Central opened in 1846 by the South Eastern Railway (SER) at Mount Pleasant and existing today on the busy main line from London to Hastings.

But for the existence of a girl who worked in Tunbridge Wells Central station refreshment room the background to a sensational bullion robbery might never have been discovered. In May 1855 three large boxes containing gold to the value of around £14,000 were robbed on the night journey from London to Paris and the contents replaced by lead bars. The boxes with the gold had been carried in padlocked iron safes, secured by Chubb locks and sealed. For a time it seemed the perfect crime.

It was more than a year later that the crime was solved – and then by accident. The ringleader was arrested on a totally unconnected charge of forgery. Before being taken inside, he asked his confederates in the bullion robbery to make sure his girlfriend,

Tunbridge Wells West station was intended as a terminus for LBSCR trains but on its opening it was linked by single track through a tunnel with Tunbridge Wells Central's SER lines. (Lens of Sutton)

68

who worked at the Tunbridge Wells refreshment room, would be looked after until he got out. But in prison he heard that the promise was not being kept so he turned Queen's Evidence and the gang were eventually brought to trial.

It transpired that the robbery had been planned by an ex-clerk from London Bridge station, the guard of the bullion train and a clerk at Folkestone. Duplicate keys of the safes were hidden in the van and during the journey some of the gold was transferred to a hold-all left as passenger luggage. This was claimed at Redhill by one member of the gang and en route to Folkestone more bags were filled. At the port the bullion boxes, now filled with lead, were transferred to the steamer and the remaining two criminals returned to London with their loot by the 1.55 am Belgian mail train. The trial exposed much detailed preparation for the robbery including a private semaphore system to indicate which train actually carried the gold.

The two Tunbridge Wells stations were once part of a race to the town. In the 1860s the LBSCR was becoming concerned at threatened incursions by the SER on its 'territory'. So a battle was on! Tunbridge Wells was first reached from East Grinstead in 1866 via Groombridge. Two years later, with the SER looking towards Lewes, the LBSCR countered with a line from Groombridge to Uckfield.

Tunbridge Wells West never became a terminus because of an Act in 1864 whereby the LBSCR and SER had agreed to cooperate over each other's tracks. So a single connecting line was built through a short tunnel after which the track curved north to join the main Hastings line towards Tunbridge Wells Central. While the West station soon became dilapidated after closure, Central station went from strength to strength. Over the years the buildings have undergone a complete face-lift and May 1986 saw the introduction of a Tonbridge–Hastings electric service.

When the LBSCR built Tunbridge Wells West station it set out to impress the local inhabitants. The buildings were quite splendid, embellished with a clock tower, a minor Big Ben, and surrounded by a louvred spirelet with a weather vane. The Carlton Hotel was built at the station's side and just beyond it a notice serving to outbid the rival SER read 'London, Brighton &

Ex-LBSCR class B4 locomotive no 2058 arrives at Groombridge in the early 1930s. (Lens of Sutton)

A Charing Cross to Hastings train, 6S unit no 1005, leaves Tunbridge Wells Central in early 1957. The narrow coaches have been built to cope with the limited bore of tunnels along the route. (Arthur Tayler)

Eridge station in pre-motoring times. This was once an important junction with lines to Eastbourne, Lewes, East Grinstead and Tunbridge Wells. (Lens of Sutton)

Eridge station with the former bay platform for trains to Tunbridge Wells West on the left. Eridge today, once a busy junction, serves trains only between the Oxted line and Uckfield. (Anthony Rispoli)

71

South Coast Railway. New Route to London: Shortest, Quickest and Most Direct. Frequent Express Trains'.

After closure of a line from Three Bridges to Groombridge in 1967, three-coach DEMUs ran a shuttle service between Eridge and Tonbridge via Groombridge and Tunbridge Wells. From Groombridge the line continued to High Rocks Halt (opened in 1907) and Tunbridge Wells West, then on through High Brooms (previously known as Southborough) to terminate at Tonbridge. The service finally ceased on 6th July 1985. In earlier years Groombridge, close to the Sussex/Kent border, had been a busy station serving four directions but towards the end only sparse traffic existed. Small wonder the line met its doom.

Spa Valley Railway

But all was not lost. A charitable society was formed to fight for the reopening of the Tunbridge Wells to Eridge line. The group named itself the Tunbridge Wells and Eridge Railway Preservation Society (TWERPS). The campaign was a long

An LBSCR 'balloon' coach at High Rocks Halt, c1910. After closure of the halt in 1952, it reopened in 1998 to serve trains on the Spa Valley Railway between Groombridge and Tunbridge Wells West. (Lens of Sutton)

A triple-header passes the site of the former High Rocks Halt on the occasion of a Spa Valley Railway Steam Gala on 9th October 2002. The train, the 1653 from Groombridge to Tunbridge Wells West, was headed by 'Lady Ingrid', 'Fonmon' and 'Spartan'. (Photograph taken by Phil Barnes)

struggle, but in the early 1990s another society acquired the line and by winter 1996 it was running trains for half a mile. The line was named as a result of a competition and so became the 'Spa Valley Railway' (SVR).

After strenuous efforts by SVR members, the line was again opened through to Groombridge, a 3 mile route and a great achievement. News spread about the route and passenger numbers rose.

A journey by a Spa Valley train can be fascinating. Starting from Tunbridge Wells the first station is High Rocks. The station, which opened in August 1998, was built by the owner of the nearby High Rocks Inn. The name derived from the ancient geological feature of the same name. At one time a Stone Age camp, there are acres of impressive sandstone outcrops which, linked together with ornamental bridges, form pleasant and unusual surroundings. The original station (High Rocks Halt) has gone but the concrete supports are still in place and can be seen from the train. The SVR station has been built a few yards to the west of the original halt.

A few minutes walk from Groombridge station there are the beautiful Groombridge Place Gardens and Enchanted Forest, designed to celebrate 'history, mystery and intrigue'. The 17th century manor here is set in a moat which dates back to 1230 and which inspired Sir Arthur Conan Doyle.

Many improvements have been made since the SVR opened, including the introduction of new steam locomotives and the building of a signal box. The engine shed at Tunbridge Wells West retains its original LBSCR 1891 design and today with its four roads houses many railway exhibits of rolling stock and motive power. There is also a souvenir shop. Tunbridge Wells West station is now a Beefeater restaurant.

Apart from numerous special events during the year, the 3 mile line is well worth a visit. Trains can be boarded at Tunbridge Wells West, High Rocks or at Groombridge. The Spa Valley Line's ambition is to extend services to Eridge where they would connect with the Uckfield line. Progress is already in hand for a new station to be built at Birchden complete with a picnic area. It will be sited just before where the SVR would join the main line into Eridge.

8
Across The Pebbles
To Dungeness

Dungeness station which closed to passenger traffic in July 1937. It was sited close to the present-day Romney, Hythe & Dymchurch Railway (RH&DR) station. (Lens of Sutton Collection)

The name Dungeness conjures up visions of lighthouses, an atomic power station and a popular narrow gauge railway. Sited close to passing shipping, a warning light of sorts has stood on the point since early in the 17th century. This was a time when an open coal fire was kept alight there, financed by dues levied on the passing vessels. Over the years the sea has receded considerably leaving the isolated marshland and pebbles.

Visitors to Dungeness Point by the Romney, Hythe & Dymchurch Railway might be excused for not being aware that,

RH&DR coach 'Gladys' serves as an observation and a bar coach. Built 1977 it is seen here at Dungeness with Dungeness lighthouse in the background. Drinks available include the new Celebration Steam Ale produced on the 75th Anniversary of the opening of the RH&DR in July 1927. (Picture courtesy Romney, Hythe & Dymchurch Railway)

almost 70 years ago, standard gauge passenger trains reached a station quite close to the RH&DR platform. Apart from a few aging posts in the ground, no other signs of the old standard gauge line really exist.

First ideas to build a railway to Dungeness came when the Rye and Dungeness Railway and Pier Company was incorporated in 1873 with grand ideas to develop the area as a train ferry terminal. Neither the railway nor the pier materialised although powers passed to the SER in 1875. In 1881 the Lydd Railway Company became involved with powers granted to build a line from Appledore to Dungeness. The nominally independent company believed that a rail link through Lydd to Appledore on the Hastings to Ashford line would provide good connections with the capital should a port be developed.

Further possibilities were foreseen. Many of the pilots and fishermen of Dungeness lived at Lydd and required transport. A large military camp was based on the outskirts of Lydd and the nearby shingle was used for testing explosives – including 'Lyddite', named after the town. The SER retained its interest in building a port. In 1881 Sir Edward Watkin, Chairman of the SER, reminded shareholders that any shingle removed from the area for use elsewhere would reduce costs in digging out a large dock system. In anticipation of such possibilities, the SER had purchased land at Dungeness for £5 an acre. But the port being considered for construction on the sheltered side of the spit was never built.

The Lydd Railway Company (to be taken over by the SER in 1895) opened its line from Appledore to Dungeness on 7th December 1881. Initially passenger trains terminated at Lydd although a goods service opened to Dungeness. Passenger services from Lydd to Dungeness followed on 19th June 1884. The branch left the Hastings to Ashford line at Appledore, then a remote village, to travel directly across Romney Marsh via Brookland Halt and Lydd. The latter was the principal station on the line with a considerable goods yard plus a long siding to

A train arrives at Lydd station, c1905 (Lydd Town from 1937). Lydd served lines to New Romney and Dungeness. (Lens of Sutton Collection)

77

army ranges. Brookland Halt was sited just over ½ mile from one of the larger villages on the marsh, an area renowned in earlier times as a centre for games and wrestling and, of course, smuggling.

Movement of shingle remained a source of traffic and it was particularly required as track ballast for the SER. Another use was the dispatch of flints to the potteries which needed them to provide the glaze. Unlike Queenborough and Port Victoria, Dungeness never got a pier and only extensive gravel pits bear witness today to the amounts railed out of the area and also the possibility that in the past a port might have been created.

Soon after the Appledore to Lydd line opened to passengers in 1881, the Lydd Railway Company gained Parliamentary approval to build a line from Appledore through Headcorn via Loose to Maidstone. The idea had been encouraged by the possibility of a port at Dungeness and, had it come about, through-trains to North Kent and beyond might have been available. Indeed it might have been possible to consider boat trains direct from London to Dungeness with a Dungeness to Boulougne crossing highly competitive to the existing Folkestone route.

All that happened was that in 1882, the following year, an Act was passed authorising construction of a branch from Lydd to New Romney. When completed in June 1884, the line, about 3 miles long, left the branch just south of Lydd to skirt the now southern perimeter of Lydd Airport. The terminus, 'New Romney and Littlestone-on-Sea', was strategically placed between the two with the idea that rail access would create a large seaside resort. Such hopes were not realised and traffic remained light throughout. There were so few trains in fact that a signal box at Romney junction was abandoned in 1911 and replaced by a ground frame.

In 1927 the Romney, Hythe & Dymchurch Railway (RH&DR) opened and by 1929 Dungeness had been reached. Although the narrow gauge trains carried mostly holidaymakers, their existence was sufficient to cause the Southern Railway to realign its New Romney branch. When completed in 1937, the new junction left the line from Lydd (renamed Lydd Town) at a point just north of Dungeness which meant that more coastal areas could be

New Romney and Littlestone-on-Sea station photographed in 1955. This was the terminus to a short branch from Lydd Town on the Dungeness branch which closed to passengers in 1967. (Stations UK)

Market day at New Romney and Littlestone-on-Sea station in the 1890s. (Lens of Sutton Collection)

79

included. Two intermediate halts were opened at Lydd-on-Sea and Greatstone-on-Sea , the latter being convenient for Greatstone Camp and Maddieson's Holiday Camp. When services on the realigned route opened, the short stretch on to Dungeness was closed.

During the Second World War, the lines did not close although obviously they went on a wartime footing. Romney Marsh was a sensitive area in the event of a German invasion and the neighbouring RH&DR was requisitioned. A mobile anti-aircraft train was constructed for the RH&DR track and trains carried troops along the line to various points of defence. Later in the war, New Romney station was used to build sections of pipeline which in 1944 were laid under the Channel to carry petrol to France. One of the pipelines ran from Dungeness to Boulogne – the route considered by the SER Chairman, Sir Edward Watkin, for his cross-Channel ferry over 60 years previously.

During the war the Southern Railway branch line distinguished itself when a train was attacked by a German bomber. According to reports, the engine, a D3 class 0-4-4T no 2365, was hit and blew up as the bomber passed low overhead causing the plane to crash. Engine 2365, an ex-LBSCR locomotive, aptly named *Victoria,* must be one of the very few, if any, to bring down an enemy aircraft.

After the war the RH&DR line needed considerable repair. The complete track was not restarted until March 1947 when filmstars Laurel and Hardy performed the opening ceremony. The last stretch from New Romney to Dungeness had been singled but this did not present any serious problems since Dungeness station was situated on a terminal loop.

The Southern Railway traffic remained virtually unaffected by the RH&DR presence and in 1952 there was an improvement in the SR services. From the previous eight daily departures from Appledore, with four to New Romney only, there were nine trains daily through to New Romney with two through from Ashford. During the summer months only, services included at least two trains each Saturday consisting of modern corridor stock directly through from Charing Cross to New Romney catering for holiday traffic.

Services continued much the same until the prohibition of steam on the South Eastern section in 1962, following electrifi-

Appledore on the Ashford to Hastings line, 1955. Trains also left Appledore for New Romney and Dungeness. (Stations UK)

Brookland Halt, 1963, looking towards Appledore. In the early 1920s the station was served by eight trains each way daily but none on Sundays. (Stations UK)

cation of the main line to Dover. From Hastings to Ashford the line remained diesel operated. Diesel-electric sets took over on the New Romney branch line and the through Saturday trains from Charing Cross stopped.

H.P. White, author of *Forgotten Railways: South East England,* recalls sight of the last steam train on 25th February 1962 on the New Romney branch. Two ex-SECR veterans, an H class 0-4-4T and a C class 0-6-0 hauled the rail tour train *Kentish Venturer* across the marsh to Appledore where 'Schools' class 30926 *Repton* was waiting.

As residential traffic dropped and freight became insignificant, the branch fell into decline. In 1963, it was listed for closure in the Beeching Report along with the Hastings to Ashford line. The following year the only significant freight

Lydd Town station, August 2002. Only the up platform and building survive. When a line first opened from Appledore in 1881, passenger trains terminated at Lydd until two years later when Dungeness was reached. (Anthony Rispoli)

traffic, delivering coal to the RH&DR, was cancelled. On 6th March 1967, the line finally closed. All that remained was a single track from Appledore to a point short of Dungeness Power Station for atomic waste to be railed in and out of the area.

Today the station building at Brookland Halt on the down platform remains as a private dwelling. At the former Lydd Town, only the up platform and building remain. The building is currently in light industrial use. As already recalled, Dungeness station is almost non-existent, the remains of a wooden platform structure being located about 50 yards west of the RH&DR station. The author could find no definite trace of the halts and stations between New Romney and Dungeness.

The Hastings to Ashford line, listed for closure in 1963, fortunately remains open to this day. After protests from the public

Brookland Halt closed to trains in March 1967 after 86 years of service. After closure of regular passenger trains it became a private residence. (Anthony Rispoli)

RH&DR 4-6-2 Pacific locomotive 'Dr Syn' at New Romney station photographed 23rd September 2001. Built in 1931, it is one of two engines on the RH&DR based on locomotives of the Canadian Pacific Railway. (John F. Bradshaw)

and local authorities alike, the Minister of Transport announced on 31st July 1974 that services would continue indefinitely. The line was never electrified but the Channel Tunnel's existence could well change this. With the line linking with Ashford it could well provide a useful link with the South Coast.

9
Trains Cross The Isle Of Grain

Allhallows-on-Sea branch opened in May 1932. The railway company hoped it would encourage a boom town for holidaymakers but this did not happen. Locomotive 31308 0-4-4T hauling a two-coach set arrives at Allhallows just before line closure. (John H. Meredith)

A visitor to the attractive resort of Allhallows-on-Sea may well wonder why the railway that served the area closed in 1961. The Southern Railway, when opening the single-track branch line from Stoke junction in 1932 was optimistic that a boom seaside resort would follow. An estate was developed with the company contributing to the cost of the railway, a pub called the British Pilot was opened and Station Hotel was built.

All was in vain since the bleak marshes did not entice the holidaymakers. Six trains a day were provided, two of these to and from London being joined or disconnected at Gravesend. Allhallows-on-Sea station comprised an island platform with a run-round loop plus carriage and goods sidings. Still hopeful, the Southern Railway doubled the track in 1935 and provided occasional Bank Holiday excursions with trains often comprising eight coaches.

Despite all efforts, attempts to sell housing plots remained unsuccessful and before long the railway authorities accepted defeat and reverted to a limited local service of push-pull trains hauled by H class 0-4-4T locomotives. As the traffic continued to deteriorate the line went back to single track in 1957. In the last year or so trains resorted to a single coach hauled by diesel locomotive. The inevitable happened and the last train, predictably packed with railway enthusiasts, ran on 4th December 1961. When the Allhallows boom town did come, comprising holiday resorts, residential caravans and houses, it was too late. The trains had gone.

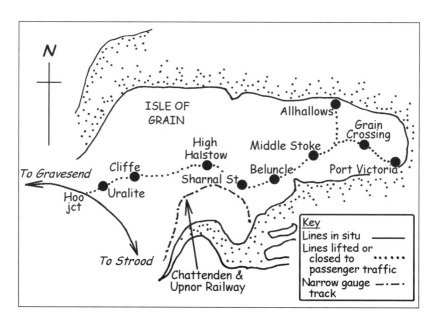

To trace the beginning of railways on the Hundred of Hoo, the peninsula between the Thames and the Medway, it is necessary to go back to 1865 when an independent company, the North Kent Extension Railway, saw the possibilities of the area. Authority was granted to build a line from the SER track at Gravesend across the marshes to a pier on the west bank of the Medway opposite Sheerness. However, since neither of the rival companies, the LCDR and the SER, liked the idea, it failed to materialise.

Origins of the railway on the peninsula go back indirectly to a Continental Trade Agreement whereby the LCDR and SER agreed to share all receipts from Kent Coast and Continental traffic in various proportions. This covered all points between Hastings and Margate but in 1876 the LCDR violated the terms by opening a railway pier at Queenborough. This was of course outside the stipulated region, nevertheless the SER was angered, although powerless to stop traffic being taken away from the agreed area.

One of the means to counter the action was for the SER to revive the scheme for a line from Gravesend to the Medway and, to achieve this end, they instigated a supposedly independent company called the Hundred of Hoo Railway Company. The SER reckoned that with the distance from Charing Cross to Port Victoria (as it was to be called) at just over 40 miles against the 52 miles on the LCDR tracks to Sheerness, they were in a strong position. Acts were agreed by 1880 and construction work began as soon as possible. In 1881 an Act was passed, predictably, authorising the SER to take over the independent company.

On 1st April 1882 the first section from Hoo junction to Sharnal Street was opened. The *Gravesend Argus* reported that 'hundreds of people of middle age saw Gravesend for the first time that day, although they had spent their lives within eight miles of it'.

Port Victoria was reached on 11th September 1882 by which time a wooden pier and a modest weatherboarded *Port Victoria Hotel* had been provided. Bearing in mind that the rival Queenborough Pier opposite was named after Philippa, wife of Edward III, the SER had gone one better and, inspired by patriotism, named their pier after the Queen.

Sharnal Street station on the Hundred of Hoo branch line which closed to passengers in 1961. (Lens of Sutton Collection)

The SER foresaw considerable traffic to the Continent and in the same year the Board of Trade approved a larger pier and powers to build docks in 1889. Neither was developed and the hoped-for trade did not materialise. When new docks were opened at Tilbury it was realised that Port Victoria had failed. It did, however, gain the advantage that it was used by royalty who appreciated its privacy and lack of road access. Queen Victoria used the route on many occasions and, prior to the First World War, it had been patronised by the German Kaiser. Other visitors of note included the King and Queen of Norway who travelled by sea and air in October 1913.

In 1898 steamer excursions to Margate were operated and in 1900 steamers reached Deal and Dover. However, the pier itself was suffering damage from attacks by marine boring worms and considerable sums were spent on repairs. When the rival companies, the LCDR and SER, merged into a joint committee in 1899 to become the SECR, much of the impetus to compete had gone. Following Queenborough Pier's destruction by fire in 1900 (the second time in 20 years), Victoria Pier unexpectedly gained the 'rival' business it had sought, although only for three months while Queenborough Pier was rebuilt.

The year 1898 saw the construction of the Chattenden & Upnor Light Railway, a 2 ft 6 ins narrow gauge line built by the War Department for army training purposes. It was built by the 8th Railway Company, Royal Engineers, who had arrived at Chattenden Barracks from Egypt in 1886. The relatively unusual gauge of 2 ft 6 ins was chosen to match up with other lines in the British Empire at that time, particularly in the North West Frontier in India. The line was completed from south of Upper Upnor with a branch from a pier at Lower Upnor to Chattenden Barracks and then to enter the Lodge Hill ammunition dump. Upnor has a long history in military activity with the nearby castle once a key point in the Medway defences. It was from here in 1667 that the Dutch fleet penetrated the Medway attacking the British fleet off Chatham to capture the *Royal Charles* which was sailed back in triumph to Holland. This was a defeat long remembered by the English.

In July 1899 the Royal Engineers left their barracks for South Africa and the Chattenden & Upnor Railway became part of a naval defence system. In 1904 railway training was transferred to Longmoor in Hampshire and the Admiralty officially adopted the line in 1906. Meantime, in 1901, a standard gauge single-track line known as the Chattenden Naval Tramway had opened covering the 2 miles from the Lodge Hill ammunition depot to Sharnal Street. This link with the SECR line provided a route into the Lodge Hill depot from Woolwich and other centres. The SECR offered to sell its Port Victoria line to the Admiralty but this was not taken up since the latter had access to the Medway by use of the Chattenden and Upnor line. The difference in gauge at Lodge Hill was not important since no through trains were required.

In 1915 the Naval Tramway was extended from Sharnal Street to Kingsnorth Pier to serve a munitions factory and airship hangars. After the First World War this standard gauge section was, rather unusually, leased to a chemical works who had taken over the munitions factory. This was one of the few occasions that a defence line was taken on by a commercial concern. In 1925 the company, Holm and Co, successfully applied for a Light

Railway Order so that passengers could be carried. In 1929 the short stretch from Sharnal Street to Kingsnorth became known as the Kingsnorth Light Railway (KLR).

By 1916 the pier at Port Victoria was once again causing serious problems. Despite previous attempts to encase the piles at the far end in concrete, it was declared unsafe and the seaward portion was barricaded off. Shortly after the end of the First World War the Royal Corinthian Yacht Club, based at Port Victoria, moved away to Burnham-on-Crouch. In 1922 Kingsferry Bridge on the Isle of Sheppey was badly damaged when struck by a Norwegian vessel and for a month or so a ferry operated between Port Victoria, Queenborough and Sheerness bringing unexpected traffic back to Port Victoria. Six years later an oil installation was established on the Isle of Grain but the pier continued to deteriorate. By 1931 no trains were allowed on it and a temporary wooden platform was built at the landward end while a basic concrete platform was completed on safer ground.

After the Second World War, much of the Isle of Grain was given over to a British Petroleum refinery plant with a station provided at Grain, opening in September 1951. Today with oil imported into the area in a refined state much of the plant and equipment has become redundant and has been dismantled. Gone too are the numerous sidings with many large areas acquiring a desolate appearance.

Initially the Port Victoria branch had only two intermediate stations, Cliffe and Sharnal Street, but new halts were added to serve villages at High Halstow, Beluncle, Middle Stoke and Grain Crossing. Between Cliffe and the junction with the Gravesend to Higham line, a halt was provided near the Uralite works used only by workmen's traffic. Uralite is an artificial material with heat-insulating qualities and is so named after asbestos imported from the Ural Mountains in Russia. When traffic dwindled after the First World War, the new branch to Allhallows-on-Sea was opened but, as already mentioned, this failed to attract sufficient passengers.

The situation lingered on until 1961, a year that was to see dramatic cut-backs to the Hundred of Hoo railways. On 19th May of that year the last service was provided on the Chattenden & Upnor Light Railway which closed officially on

High Halstow Halt on the single-lined branch from Hoo junction to Port Victoria. This remote halt, situated between Cliffe and Sharnal Street, opened in July 1906 to encourage local traffic. It was photographed just before closure in 1961. (Stations UK)

Two-coach unit 1682 arrives at Port Victoria terminus on 6th December 1947. The train, a midday Saturday motor-train unit, comprised one ex-LSWR coach and one ex-SECR coach. (John H. Meredith)

Locomotive no 31308 takes on water on the middle road at Gravesend Central in November 1961. The picture was taken two weeks before closure of the Allhallows branch on 4th December 1961. (John H. Meredith)

31st December 1961. In the same year the Lodge Hill to Sharnal Street standard gauge link closed – the line to Kingsnorth had closed in 1940. On 4th December 1961 passenger services from Hoo junction on the Gravesend line to Grain and the branch to Allhallows finally ground to a halt. All that remained was the single track line from Hoo junction across the peninsula to Port Victoria plus numerous sidings for industrial purposes.

Perhaps one of the best places to imagine the past is at the site of Sharnal Street station where the A228 crosses two bridges in the valley. The single track still exists on the line to Port Victoria and the station was situated on the north-west side of an adjoining track at the end of a slope. The station buildings have gone but rough concrete foundations show their position. The second bridge crossed the track (now removed) to Kingsnorth and, in the other direction, the Chattenden Naval Tramway linked with the Lodge Hill armoury.

Port Victoria, July 1951. Train services were suspended shortly after this photograph was taken. The pipeline seen on the right was used for conveying silt to reclaim land for the Grain Oil Refinery. (John H. Meredith)

The Allhallows branch can be traced largely by the lines of hedgerows marking the trackbed across the open area. At All-hallows, the station has gone to be replaced by homes in an area called Willow Close. Station Hotel has become a block of flats called Avery Court and the only evidence that a railway existed is that for many years a solitary water-tower has stood incongruously amid the caravans in the Kingsmead Holiday Camp.

10
Gravesend West –
A Port And A Station

The Town Pier at Gravesend, formerly the 'station' for the London, Tilbury & Southend Railway which operated a ferry service from 1854. (Picture courtesy Gravesham Borough Council)

When a five mile line from Fawkham junction to Gravesend opened to public traffic on 10th May 1886, barricades were erected across the approach to the station in Stuart Road in an attempt to stop the trains from running. The action was taken by Lord Darnley, a notable landowner, who disputed the LCDR's right to use his roads in the town. Fortunately for the railway

94

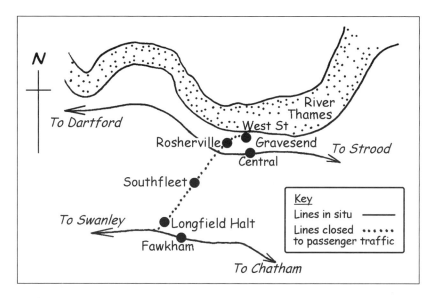

authorities, the matter was resolved and the barricades were removed by workmen just half an hour before the first train was due to depart.

The double-track line to Gravesend from Fawkham junction on the Swanley to Chatham line was another classic example of a railway duplicating existing services with no real hope of success. Proposals were first considered by the Gravesend Railway Co, an off-shoot of the LCDR, early in 1881. At the same time, the SER, aware of the scheme, was considering a line from Snodland to Northfleet which would take up the land required by the Gravesend (LCDR) company. The latter successfully petitioned against this and its own Bill received Royal Assent on 18th July 1881.

Various ideas were put forward as to a location for the terminus and finally Stuart Street was adopted. A further plan to build a branch from the outskirts of Gravesend to Northfleet never materialised. In July 1882 the company was authorised to build a pier and a short section of track to connect trains with steamers. During construction the Gravesend Railway Co was taken over by the LCDR.

Justification for the line was difficult to find. Gravesend had

*Gravesend's West Pier for passengers using the Tilbury-Gravesend Ferry.
Photographed in April 1961. (Picture A.E. Bennett/Gravesham Borough
Council)*

been reached in 1849 when the SER North Kent line opened and
further potential competition came in 1854 when the London,
Tilbury & Southend Railway (LTSR) started a ferry service to
Gravesend from its Tilbury station on the opposite bank of the
Thames. This was worked as an extension to its Fenchurch Street
service and proved very competitive in time and cost. In 1881 the
LTSR planned a tunnel under the Thames, possibly to link with
the Gravesend tracks, but the idea was dropped probably
through lack of finance.

In 1860 the LCDR came on the scene with its service from
Bickley to Rochester Bridge and it was from this line that the
Gravesend West branch struck northwards from Fawkham junc-
tion at a point marked only by a solitary signal box between
Farningham Road and Fawkham stations. The branch, which
ran through a prolific market garden area, was formally opened

on 17th April 1886. The date coincided with the opening of Tilbury Docks, thought to be a futile gesture by the LCDR to draw attention away from the new dock services. In fact, the same official opening party attended both events, the occasion concluding with a celebration party at the New Falcon Hotel in Gravesend. Despite the legal formalities it was another three weeks or so before a passenger service started.

One of the attractions along the line was the Rosherville Pleasure Gardens which had opened in 1840, then served by steamers from the river. In 1886 on Whit Monday alone, some 14,000 people visited the gardens, many using the new branch line and its station at Rosherville. The pleasure steamers did not give up their passengers lightly and undercut the rail fares. Unfortunately for both methods of travel, the garden was already declining in popularity and closure came in 1900. It was reopened in 1903 to finally close in 1910. The station survived, even though passengers were few, and did not close until July 1933.

Initially the Gravesend West branch was served by fourteen

The imposing entrance to the former Gravesend West Street station buildings taken before final closure of the branch to goods in 1968. (Picture courtesy Gravesham Borough Council)

trains each way on weekdays and eight on Sundays. All trains ran through from London with a journey time of about 70 minutes. When a working agreement came between the LCDR and the SER to become the SECR in 1899, the only change was that 'Gravesend (C&D)' became known as Gravesend West Street station to distinguish if from the 'Gravesend (SER)' station which became Gravesend Central.

On 1st July 1913 Longfield Halt opened, situated in a chalk cutting and built of wood with access by staircases from the overbridge. The opening was part of a drive by the SECR to cut costs and increase traffic, an exercise which included the introduction of push-pull trains, initially worked by H class 0-4-4Ts with ex-SER four-wheeled coaches. It was clear the line was now more a branch rather than, as previously, an extension of the main line.

In 1916 during the First World War the Dutch Batavia line rather unexpectedly introduced a regular service from Gravesend West Street Pier to Rotterdam. To back this up, the railway began regular boat trains from Victoria to meet the sailings and at

Longfield Halt on the Gravesend West branch line. The halt opened on 1st July 1913 as part of a drive by the SECR to cut costs and increase traffic. (Lens of Sutton Collection)

The pier end of Gravesend West Street station before closure to passengers in 1953. The covered-way was built during World War I to accommodate passengers walking from train to ferry. (Lens of Sutton Collection)

Gravesend West Street station a wooden covered way was constructed to link the station with the pier so that ferry passengers could walk from train to boat completely under cover. Perhaps the service's main claim to fame was its occasional use by the Crown Prince of Holland as a discreet means to cross the North Sea and therefore more secure than the popular LNER route via Harwich.

Fruit and agricultural products made up much of the freight carried mostly from Southfleet. Autumn soft fruit featured prominently and a waybill issued in September 1934 showed over 5 cwt of blackberries consigned to a 'Mr Lamb of Bradford (LNE Rly G N Section) at a cost of £1.13.11d'. It was a time of the year when fruit pickers came from London in the same way that others went hop picking. Special trains were run and pickers were accommodated in camps, one of which was near Longfield.

In July 1939 both the main routes across the area were electrified but the Gravesend West branch was not considered of sufficient importance. To get current from the Central Electricity Board at Northfleet to Fawkham junction, a cable was laid alongside the line although ironically the cable never fed the track. Two months

99

later war broke out leading to the inevitable closure of the Batavia Shipping line to the Netherlands. At the same time services were reduced to five trains each way daily but with an increased service on Saturdays, mostly for shoppers, and no trains on Sundays.

After the war, the Batavia line restarted its services but this time using Tilbury across the river with its better facilities. In 1950 further changes followed. Gravesend West Street station became simply Gravesend West and the period saw the use of the pier by the General Steam Navigation running pleasure trips along the river.

Freight traffic had now reduced to a trickle and passenger services were suffering badly from competition by local bus services. Passenger services were withdrawn on 3rd August.1953 but for the next few years a daily goods train continued to run the line. In 1959 the track was singled and Longfield Halt plus Southfleet station buildings and platforms were removed. By 1961 class 33 diesel-electrics had replaced the long-serving class C locomotives.

In September 1962 a local paper agitated for the single-line branch to be electrified and limited passenger services restarted with trains possibly splitting at Swanley Junction and running a four-coach unit to Gravesend. However, the Beeching cuts were not far off and the branch closed to goods traffic on 24th March 1968 – but not before a train entered Gravesend West station carrying 350 members of the Locomotive Club of Great Britain. It was the first passenger train to travel the line since 1953.

Final closure was followed by the lifting of a short section of track north of Southfleet. The track from Fawkham junction to Southfleet remained in use for a number of years to be used by APCM (Blue Circle Industries) which established a coal depot in the area.

The entire area where once Gravesend West station and pier existed has given way to development. Today only the ghosts of the past walk down where a covered way existed from the station platform to board a ship bound for the Continent. The walkway had been built during the First World War to shelter intending passengers from bad weather. There were hopes in the 1980s that the branch might become a preserved railway but these did not materialise. The branch had survived 82 years for passengers and then goods traffic. It was a line built through competition between earlier railway companies that was never justified.

This aerial view of the former Gravesend West railway station site was taken in the 1980s. It is possible to trace the station's position by the curve leading away from the pier edge. (Picture courtesy Gravesham Borough Council)

11
The Elham Valley Railway

Elham railway station which opened in July 1887 comprising numerous sidings and a level crossing. (Lens of Sutton Collection)

It is hard to realise when visiting the attractive Elham Valley that a railway line that for a time had main line status once passed through the area. Much of the original trackbed has been lost either to modern development or overgrown by the passage of time. However, for the enthusiast there are still many relics to be found giving evidence of the line that closed almost 60 years ago.

Off the B2065 at Etchinghill, the tunnel under Teddars Lee Road can still be located although it is partly hidden by trees and shrubs. Not far away Lyminge station buildings have survived as a public library. All that remains of Elham station is a platform edge at the side of a path that was once the 'up' track. The area south of the platform, where a signal box once stood proudly, was strongly defended by a flock of geese when visited by the author not too long ago!

Any stop at Elham would not be complete without a visit to the ragstone and flint church of St Mary the Virgin which dates back to the late 15th century. Not far from the former station can be found the Abbot's Fireside Hotel, a remarkable example of pre-Renaissance architecture built during the 15th century, where welcome refreshment or perhaps even a longer stay can be enjoyed. The whole building leans slightly forward, adding to the hotel's air of 'olde worlde' charm.

Leaving Elham it is not difficult to follow the line of the track 4 miles northwards to Barham. A road bridge stands along the route but at Barham itself the abutments of a bridge have survived for many years on a road west from the B2065. A local resident proudly claimed that his rear garden in Heathfield Close was once Barham station platform. Bishopsbourne and Bridge stations still exist but these are strictly private residences. Finally came Canterbury South station which was lost to

Lyminge station opened in 1887 was to last 60 years. The building is used today as a public library. (Lens of Sutton Collection)

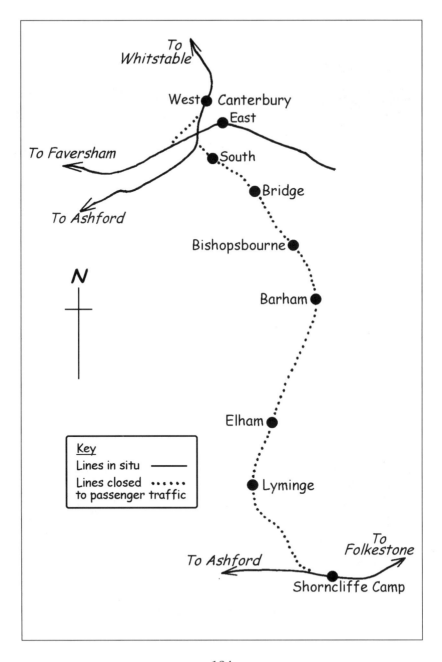

Barham served as a terminus for two years from the Folkestone line until Canterbury was reached in 1889. (Lens of Sutton Collection)

A lone passenger poses for the camera at Canterbury South station on the Elham Valley branch in 1936. When the station opened it was named 'South Canterbury'. (Stations UK)

building development over 20 years ago. The station was situated behind houses in South Canterbury Road and along the trackbed to the east now stands Kent and Canterbury Hospital.

First serious ideas for a railway from the South Coast between Hythe and Folkestone towards Canterbury came in 1865 when a group of wealthy landowners presented a prospectus to Parliament. The proposal was to build a single track line from Hythe across to Newington then north-westwards through a 660 yard tunnel at Etchinghill and along the Nail Bourne Valley to eventually join the LCDR Canterbury to Dover line opened in 1861. The scheme ran into many financial difficulties and the company was dissolved in 1873.

No doubt tempted by the plan for this additional route, the LCDR floated its own ideas. Plans were considered for a new line linking Canterbury and Folkestone leaving the Dover line at Kearsney then progressing along the valley via Alkham. Not only would this increase LCDR business but also compete very effectively against the existing SER line from Folkestone to Dover which had been suffering badly from landslips due to crumbling chalk.

The proposal rang serious alarm bells for the SER which felt this to be a direct involvement in its 'territory' and in consequence plans were drawn up in 1879 to extend its own network through the Elham Valley, frustrating any LCDR move. The idea was to construct a single-line railway from Cheriton to join the tracks just south of Canterbury on the line from Ashford. This project was dropped the following year due to difficulties in purchasing the necessary land and because of objections from the Board of Trade.

The SER persisted and in 1881 a modified plan was presented called the Elham Valley Light Railway Company Bill which received Royal Assent to proceed. Still nothing further happened until three years later the rival LCDR followed up its Alkham Valley project with a station planned at Shorncliffe (Folkestone West). The LCDR further angered the SER by proposing to continue the line from Shorncliffe to London by running parallel to the SER track.

In his book *The Elham Valley Line – 1887 to 1947*, Brian Hart writes of the emotions between the two railway companies which had now reached a high level. Folkestone was plastered with hundreds of posters by the rival companies, each proclaiming the merits of its own line and each making the most slanderous accusations against the other. In order to establish its own case the SER assumed ownership of the Elham Valley Light Railway Co (EVLR) and agreed to build the line as double track and to the same standard as its existing main line. Parliament approved the SER bill by an Act dated 1884 with the consequence that the company was now faced with building a main line through an area which offered poor financial return.

With the way at last clear, plans were drawn up to build the line in two stages. The stretch from Cheriton junction (on the main Folkestone line) to Barham would be constructed first with the remainder to follow. Thomas Walker was appointed

The abutments of a bridge which once carried Elham Valley trains to be found a short distance from the Peene Elham Valley Railway Museum. (Anthony Rispoli)

engineer and surveys along the route commenced, much to the delight of the village folk. The official ceremony of 'cutting the first sod' took place at Peene near Newington (just north of Cheriton junction) on 28th August 1884 with large numbers present. The Mayor of Folkestone attended and Sir George Russell, Chairman of the EVLR, gave a spirited speech before picking up the special spade mounted in silver to cut the first sod. After the National Anthem, a sumptuous luncheon followed for almost 200 guests.

During construction there was a petition presented by the villagers of Newington requesting a station on the new line. The SER deferred the matter and it was conveniently dropped. Meanwhile at Lyminge local farmers were objecting to a level-crossing proposed immediately to the south of the station, claiming it was dangerously situated. The SER upheld its claim and a bridge was built on Nash Hill for the princely sum of £500. At Elham it was the reverse. Villagers objected to a bridge across Duck Street so a level-crossing was provided.

Eventually the first part of the line to Barham was completed and the first train ran on Monday, 4th July 1887. Although there was no official opening ceremony, villagers turned out in large numbers to cheer the train's arrival. It left Shorncliffe at 8.05 am to arrive at Barham at 8.22 am with stops at Lyminge and Elham.

Prior to the opening there had been much speculation about the section of line from Barham to Canterbury with claims, particularly in the local press, that the route would not be completed. It had been revealed that, up to a late stage, the SER still had to purchase land on the remaining section and agreement with many landowners was still required. Indeed one press report claimed that the northern section would be constructed by the LCDR and the whole line worked jointly.

This of course did not happen but problems with obstinate landowners were hard to overcome. The most difficult situation was at Bourne Park between Bishopsbourne and Bridge. The owner, Matthew Bell, refused adamantly to accept the planned siting of the track and would not agree to the prospect of seeing trains pass by the rear of his mansion. After much delay, the SER reluctantly agreed to build a tunnel instead of two bridges to keep the trains from view. Work on the Bourne Park tunnel commenced in late 1887 and took some eighteen months to complete with the cost of three lives due to earth slips and accidents. With the tunnel completed Matthew Bell's eldest son requested a station to serve Bishopsbourne. The SER not surprisingly agreed only on the understanding that land for such a station would be given free.

It was planned that the northern end of the line would cross the LCDR line between Canterbury East and Faversham to join the existing SER line south of Canterbury West. No doubt dismayed at the heavy earthworks at the northern end, it was at this point that certain of the press claims over involvement with the LCDR became justified. Edward Watkin, the SER Chairman, wrote in September 1888 to the rival company suggesting a junction where the lines crossed but after consideration the LCDR rejected the idea. Had it happened, of course, the Elham Valley branch line might have taken on a new significance since a new direct route between Folkestone and Victoria would have come about.

The final obstacle to completing the entire length was the building of a 72 ft girder bridge across the Great Stour but once this was finished the track was joined to the Ashford-Canterbury West line at Harbledown junction. An official train completed the journey on 24th June 1889 carrying the directors of the EVLR and the SER. A week later on 1st July 1889 a public service began with six trains each way daily with Sundays included. Return fares were 5s 2d for first class, 3s 10d for second class and 2s 8d for third class over the line which was nearly 17 miles long.

The branch line diverged from the main Folkestone to Ashford line at Cheriton junction. After negotiating the tunnel at Etchinghill the line entered the Elham Valley to reach Lyminge. Lyminge and Elham stations were conveniently sited for the villages. Barham and Bishopsbourne followed, also well placed, but northwards the line began to climb the valley side where Bridge was remote from the village centre. The last station on the branch was Canterbury South, not far from Canterbury itself, although little traffic was generated locally into the town.

For many years the Elham Valley saw Cudworth 118 class locomotives with Q class 0-4-4Ts becoming prominent together with O class 0-6-0s. In 1899 the old rivals LCDR and SER entered

Looking northwards at Bridge station, 1936. After closure in 1947 the station building became a private residence. (Stations UK)

a working union to be known as the South Eastern & Chatham Railway (SECR) although the official title was South Eastern & Chatham Railway Companies Managing Committee. This had virtually no effect on the line except that the station lamp-posts and nameboards were eventually repainted in buff and reddish brown.

The summer of 1913 saw the first introduction of railmotors although these were confined to services between Folkestone and Elham only. They were not totally successful with the train taking almost twice as long to climb the 1 in 90 gradient up to Etchinghill. Around the same time non-stop trains from Canterbury to Folkestone were introduced taking 25 minutes for the 'down' journey but 5 minutes longer on the 'up' line.

When war came in 1914 the branch was taken over by the military. This involved considerable troop movements and use by Red Cross trains. By 1916 much of the track was being used for storage of ammunition and other wartime goods, so single-line working was introduced. The line increased in importance when on 19th December 1915 there was a massive landslip at Folkestone Warren. Such was the scale of the disaster that an

A reminder of SECR days can be found with this crest on the gates of the Elham Valley Railway Museum at Peene, Newington, near Folkestone. At the museum many artefacts and memorabilia of the past can be enjoyed. (Anthony Rispoli)

A train awaits departure at Bishopsbourne station, 1936. The line, opened in 1889, was singled in the First World War, reinstated afterwards, but singled again in 1931. (Stations UK)

engine and four coaches sank into the moving chalk and the track was badly damaged for over a mile. Happily there were no casualties but due to the extent of the disruption, the SECR closed the Dover to Folkestone line for the remainder of the war. Trains now travelling from one port to the other had to use a lengthy diversion via Deal, Minster, Canterbury and the Elham Valley.

When hostilities came to an end in 1918 the SECR built a link between the Ashford-Ramsgate and the Faversham-Dover lines, a move that would have been strongly resisted by the rival companies some 30 years previously. With the Warren line still closed, this meant Dover to Folkestone trains could bypass Deal and Minster by a more direct route although a reversal was necessary.

In the early 1930s the effects of 'motor omnibuses' were beginning to be felt. With a good road running parallel to most of the branch (B2065), the Southern Railway, formed following

Southern Railway locomotive no 1161 photographed at Lyminge on 24th May 1947. After the Second World War attempts were made to revive passenger traffic on the Elham Valley branch but there was little success. (John H. Meredith)

grouping in 1923, announced that the line would be singled. This was carried out in 1931 between Harbledown junction and Lyminge with the remainder to Cheriton staying as before. At the same time appropriate staff reductions were taking place. With traffic on the decline, few people were surprised.

During the Second World War the line took on greater significance when used by an 18 inch railway gun called *Boche Buster*. This was designed as a defence weapon capable of firing shells weighing 1¼ tons over a range of some 12 miles. It could only fire parallel to the track but the curving line meant it could cover most of the Kent coast in the possible event of invasion. It was ironic that the gun should occasionally find shelter in Bourne tunnel, an earthwork so strongly resisted during construction over 50 years previously.

After the war the railway returned to passenger and goods traffic but both were poorly patronised. In 1947 the inevitable happened and despite pleas from the local inhabitants, passenger services were withdrawn from 14th June and goods by 10th October. For many it was a sad ending to a fine branch line that had lasted 60 years.

12
The Chatham Central Branch And A Canal

Higham station in SER days photographed in the early 1880s. In the distance the entrance to Higham tunnel. (Lens of Sutton Collection)

It seems incredible to think that rivalry between railway companies in the late 19th century led to a situation where two bridges crossed the river Medway, side by side, each carrying trains in the same direction. The problem arose in 1891/2 when the SER duplicated a service already in existence by the LCDR in an effort to capture Chatham traffic.

The line was so extravagant to build and so little used that the short branch, about a mile long, became a white elephant almost on completion. Construction involved a railway bridge, built to an unnecessarily high standard, and new stations not far from the existing LCDR track.

First trains to reach Strood came from Gravesend in 1848. The track was single and initially worked in conjunction with a canal

114

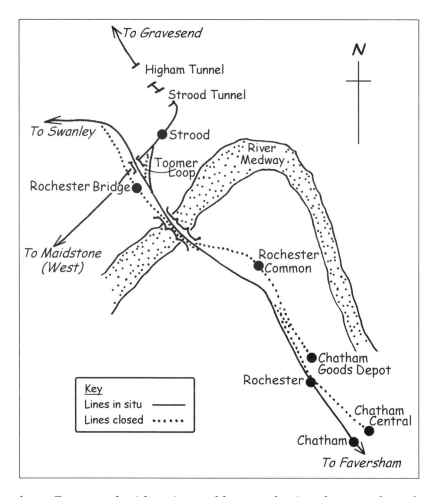

from Gravesend with trains and barges sharing the tunnel north of Strood. Within a year the SER took over the line, abandoned the canal and doubled the track.

A waterway across Kent had first been proposed around 1800 when consideration had been given to linking the river Thames at Gravesend with the harbour of Rye in East Sussex. The project never materialised but the Thames and Medway Canal between Gravesend and Frindsbury certainly became a reality. Initial estimates for the 7 mile stretch were put at around £25,000 but when it finally opened some 24 years later it cost more than ten times as much.

The whole Thames and Medway Canal project was beset with difficulties. Its purpose was to save a passage of some 47 miles on the original route round the Isle of Grain. Ralph Dodd, an engineer, reckoned that the vast amounts of chalk to be excavated could be sold to reduce costs and he expected subsequent trade at over 65,000 tons a year. At first no tunnelling was anticipated and long cuttings were planned removing some 600,000 cubic yards of chalk. Dodd consulted engineer John Rennie who considered a tunnel would be more substantial although the estimate now increased to £57,500 including a lock and basin at each end.

Work began in 1800 and by the end of 1801 four miles had been completed from Gravesend to Higham. Doubts soon arose over the route. It was realised that by waiting for suitable tides and with delays at locks, little time would be gained since barges could reach Chatham from Gravesend on the sea route as quickly as those coming through the canal! Changes were made and it is thought that by this time Dodd had left. His departure was no doubt accelerated by his failure over a Thames tunnel, the Gravesend shaft of which remained abandoned after expenditure of some £15,000.

Work on the canal stood still until early in 1808 when new interest was shown. Fresh contractors were appointed and excavation in the canal tunnel started in April 1819. Expenses were mounting, frequently because of compensation payable to difficult landowners; even so within six months progress had been made. The tunnel, now becoming an object of curiosity with many visitors, was claimed to be the longest in Britain, 3,931 yards in length. Probably for the first time an astronomer's telescope, mounted in an observatory that commanded a view over the whole site, was used to lay out the tunnel line and select where shafts should be sunk.

Tunnelling was done from each end and from nine working shafts where men and materials were moved by horse-operated rums or whims. Some of the chalk was so compacted that gunpowder had to be used to break it up. These sections remained unlined but where chalk was loose, brick lining of various thicknesses had to be built. A towpath was provided through the tunnel and later an iron railing was added for safety. Money ran out frequently before completion. Much of the expenditure had been due to an unexpected amount of brick arching required. Further loans were made and finally, amid great celebrations, the tunnel was finished on 14th October 1824. The canal was 7 miles long, 51 ft wide at the top surface and 7 ft deep except in the tunnel. It could take 60 ton sailing barges measuring 94 ft 8 in by 22 ft 8 in.

Problems arose through loss of water in the tunnel. In the early years 4 inches could be lost each 24 hours and eventually, to supplement filling by tides, a steam engine was installed at Gravesend to pump through additional water. This proved expensive. In one year alone it worked 3,666 hours, used 444 tons of coal and cost £520 to run, not including wages. The total cost of the canal at opening could now be assessed at about £260,000 against the original figure of £25,000.

Delays occurred, however, at peak times through boats needing to pass each other in the tunnel. Business had improved so some money could now be spent to open out a passing place near the tunnel centre. This was completed in 1830 at an approximate cost of £13,000. The sides of the opening stood perpendicular about 100 ft high and have remained so ever since.

The two tunnels, as they now were, proved popular with visitors who walked through them, rowed to them (the Canal Tavern, Gravesend, hired boats) or went there on pleasure trips. According to Charles Hadfield in his book *Canals of South and South East England*, there was great excitement when the steamboat *Adelaide* passed through the canal. It is said that 'in the tunnel torches were used to throw their lurid glare. The vessel almost filled the channel and the passengers, with the noise of the paddles, the indistinct light and a consciousness of traversing the bowels of the earth, experienced a very odd and certainly novel sensation. . .'

In the 1830s the hop business and general trade along the canal remained busy but serious competition from the railways was on the way. As the trains progressed, the canal owners were forced to a situation where they had little choice but to sell to the

For most of 1845 trains ran alongside barges through the Higham and Strood tunnels on the Thames and Medway Canal. (Ironbridge Gorge Museum Trust/Elton Collection)

railways. This happened on 8th February 1844, when the company became the Gravesend and Rochester Railway and Canal Company. Soon a single track railway was built through the tunnel on a line from Gravesend to Strood with one rail laid on the towpath and the other supported from the side of the canal bed.

Many people thought it would be dangerous to run trains through the canal tunnel so a Board of Trade inspection was arranged. Major Pasley did his job thoroughly. He went through with a team at night on a barge carrying a special inspection bridge and fired small blank mortars at the chalk to see if he could shift it! Fortunately for the team it didn't happen and he pronounced the walls and roof safe. The line should have opened on 23rd January 1845, but a pay dispute held it up. Workmen took possession of a station and threatened to blow it up if their demands were not met. It was finally settled by arbitration and a service began on 10th February. Engine chimneys were fitted with shields to deflect the smoke and

Steam trains in abundance at Chatham station in the early 1920s. Chatham on the line from Faversham to Swanley was opened by the East Kent Railway Company (LCDR from 1859) in 1858. (Lens of Sutton Collection)

carriages had barred windows on the towpath side of the tunnels. For 18 months trains and barges operated side by side.

In August 1846 the company was bought by the SER. The canal from Higham to Strood was filled in and double track was laid. Ten years later, in 1856, SER trains from Strood had reached Maidstone.

Meantime the East Kent Railway (EKR) was consolidating territory with a new line opened from Chatham to Faversham in January 1858. Since the Swanley to Chatham line had no physical link with the SER Strood station, and since an Act of 1853 gave the EKR the right to use this station, a short branch from Chatham to Strood was completed two months later on 29th March 1858. By 1860 the EKR, known as the London, Chatham & Dover Railway from 1859, completed a further line from Rochester Bridge to St Mary Cray where it joined the Mid-Kent line thus giving access to the West End of London.

With this new route in operation, the traffic on the short branch from Chatham to Strood dwindled to occasional goods

Rochester Bridge station originally built on the LCDR line to Victoria was opened in 1860 and closed in January 1917. (Lens of Sutton Collection)

traffic particularly since the LCDR wanted as little to do with the SER as possible. As far as the SER was concerned, all it could do at the time was operate a competitive horse-bus service.

It was at this point that Alderman Toomer made his name in history by his frequent complaints of the inadequate service offered. The Alderman, then Mayor of Rochester, complained to the Railway Commission in 1876. The Commission was sympathetic but Alderman Toomer had to keep up considerable pressure and it was not until the following year that satisfactory services to Strood were restarted. Since that time the spur has been referred to as the 'Toomer Loop'.

The situation now appeared satisfactory to all but the SER. Still anxious to capture Chatham traffic, the company gained authorisation to build a line to the town. Unfortunately for the promoters, the company was now going through a period of financial restraint and it was not until 1888 that the powers were revived. A line opened from Strood to Rochester Common station in July 1891 and Chatham Central station (actually closer to Rochester) was reached on 1st March 1892. From Strood the line was built parallel to the Toomer Loop and then it crossed the Medway by the extravagant railway bridge that is still used today.

120

The branch was soon to see economies with the introduction of railcar units in 1905. The units, although able to give a frequent and usually reliable service, were never really popular. Carriages were less comfortable and often smoky and covered with ash. Railcar no 2 worked the Chatham–Strood service from February 1905, probably from new. It stayed for two years before moving on to Hastings when other railcar units took over. By 1910 P class 0-6-0T locomotives were taking their place and one of these was no 323 which is now *Bluebell* on the well-known preserved railway of the same name.

The farcical situation over the similar services lasted only 19 years. In 1899 the authorities realised the folly of the two lines and by 1911 the old SER line was closed. The original LCDR section (the Toomer Loop) was abandoned and, following connections between the tracks at the Rochester end of the bridge, the SER loop was used. The Toomer Loop had its last moment of glory when a fire damaged the SER bridge and trains were diverted back along it for the three years it took to complete repairs.

In 1927 track alterations were made to ease the curve from the Sole Street direction. Because of this, the original Toomer Loop was lost and trains were confined to the present-day bridge. Although the LCDR bridge was strengthened during the Second World War in case of possible bombing, it was eventually demolished to make way for a new road bridge.

Today, Chatham Central station has gone and with it the only intermediate station on the SER line, called Rochester Common. The foundations of the old LCDR railway bridge were utilised when a road bridge (today the A2) was built in the 1960s. The sharp curve from the river to Strood is still occasionally referred to as the Toomer Loop even though this is not strictly correct. By the end of 2003 a further bridge will cross the Medway. This will carry trains on the Channel Tunnel Rail Link (CTRL) between Ashford and Fawkham junction en route to Waterloo.

Earlier in this chapter mention was made of an opening cut out in 1830 in the tunnel between Strood and Higham. The only indication of this today is that a railway passenger travelling on the line may well notice a brief flash of daylight halfway through the tunnel. It was at this spot that barges used to pass each other over 160 years ago.

13
The Hoppers' Line
To Hawkhurst

Hawkhurst station looking towards the buffers, May 1949. The station was not built as a terminus since it was anticipated that the branch line would continue southwards but this never materialised. (John H. Meredith)

The first train from Paddock Wood left for Goudhurst on 1st October 1892, with its locomotive, a Cudworth E class 2-4-0, wreathed in bunting. It was a ceremonial affair and a public service between the two towns followed the next day. By 1893 the branch had been completed and trains reached Hawkhurst at the end of the line.

First ideas for such a route came in 1864 when the SER obtained powers to build a line from Paddock Wood to Cranbrook and a nominally independent Weald of Kent Company was incorporated to extend the line to Hythe via Tenterden and Shorncliffe, a distance of about 25 miles. One of the reasons for such a line was to compete against the rival LCDR but with the LCDR soon to find itself in serious financial trouble, the threat was removed and the SER's proposal was dropped for the time being.

Another attempt to build came in 1877 when an independent concern, the Cranbrook and Paddock Wood Railway Company, revived the scheme. But SER support was dependent upon £25,000 being raised locally and with such funds not available the idea was dropped once more. Despite the setback the company persisted, considering the hop trade alone as sufficient incentive to build a line. As if to emphasise its faith in the future, the private company displayed a bunch of hops on its seal.

In 1882 powers were granted to extend the proposed line from Cranbrook to Hawkhurst. Matters still dragged on until an SER Act of 1887 gained government approval. Finally an Amendment of 1892 proposed that the section between Goudhurst and Hawkhurst should be built on a 'cost saving' basis. The Cranbrook and Paddock Wood Company was eventually absorbed by the SER in 1900.

Paddock Wood station first opened in 1842 when it was an intermediate stop on the Tonbridge to Ashford (SER) line. At first the station was called Maidstone Road but two years later it was renamed Paddock Wood. It was then still an area of virtually no significance and its name came from a nearby woodland. Industry soon followed and with it many housing estates. Just north of the station is a pub called the Hop Pocket (a pocket is an outsize sack) as a reminder of earlier prosperity.

The branch line had three intermediate stations at Horsmonden, Goudhurst and Cranbrook. Horsmonden is an attractive village with weatherboarded houses and pubs built round a small triangle that was once the village pound. Small wonder it has earned in the past the title 'Best Kept Village of Kent'. On closure of the line the station site, to the east of the village, became a garage and, where trucks once stood in a small siding, cars await repair. Overlooking the garage stands a tall 18th century building called Station House, once the home of the station master.

Goudhurst, where the station was first known as 'Hope Mill for Goudhurst and Lamberhurst', is not far to the south. The village stands on a summit of land and railway travellers faced a stiff climb from the station. The efforts of visitors were surely rewarded as they passed attractive half-timbered tile-hung and weatherboarded houses interspersed with a number of welcoming tearooms. At the top of the hill on the right stands the Star and Eagle, thought at one time to have had monastic connections with the adjacent church.

There was a church at Goudhurst as early as 1117. The present building was enlarged in the 14th century when the population grew with the influx of weavers from Flanders. The tower was destroyed in a storm in 1637 but was replaced by the present stocky structure which, being over 500 ft above sea level, was used as a lookout point in both World Wars.

Goudhurst station lay to the west of the village next to the Green Cross public house. Perhaps one of the station's claims to fame was when it starred in the 1950s in a children's TV serial called *The Old Pull and Push*. Today almost all trace has gone and the area is privately owned. The only indication that trains once stopped there is the fact that the house is called Haltwhistle and old station lights line the drive.

Goudhurst station not long before closure of the line in 1961. The station, which stood close to where today's Green Cross Inn can be found, was completely cleared after closure and a house built where the goods yard once existed. (R.K. Blencowe)

124

The remains of Goudhurst station well after closure. In the 1950s the station claimed fame when it was used in a children's TV serial 'The Old Pull and Push'. (John F. Bradshaw)

The site of Cranbrook station can be found a short distance down a narrow road opposite the Duke of York public house. Here the single platform and the elegant station master's house were remote indeed from the town, being more than 2 miles walk away. After closure the station became Cranbrook Pottery with many fine samples for sale. But today all this has gone and, although the station master's house is well preserved, the platform building became derelict.

Hawkhurst at the end of the line perhaps reached its height of fame, or rather notoriety, as a town in the first half of the 18th century. This was when the 'Hawkhurst Gang' of smugglers held a reign of terror over much of Kent and Sussex. They regularly murdered or tortured opponents and were so self-assured that frequently after successful smuggling runs to Rye, they would celebrate at the Mermaid Inn with their loaded pistols lying on the table in front of them without any interference from the magistrates.

125

Cranbrook station on the Hawkhurst branch line, 1961. The station closed to goods and passenger traffic in June 1961 to become a private residence. (Stations UK)

By the time the railways arrived, Hawkhurst led a more peaceful existence. The station, like many in Kent, was situated some distance from the village, over a mile to the north at Gills Green. For a time it had two platforms but the second rarely accommodated a train. Despite this, Hawkhurst boasted an engine shed, a goods yard and many sidings. It was never really built as a terminus and construction left the option of an extension southwards although of course this never materialised.

A feature of the line was that, although station masters were provided with ample three-storey buildings, the travelling public had to be satisfied with rather basic corrugated iron structures which included waiting rooms and ticket offices. They were single-storey buildings with their roofs extended onto wooden posts at the front to form canopies.

As expected, the line was soon busy with hops, the traditional crop of the area. The railway assisted in the annul invasion of mid-Kent by thousands of poorer working class families, mostly from the East End of London. Whole families picked hops by day

126

and slept by night in the numerous 'hopper-huts' provided in lines by the fields. For many this was their annual holiday. In the evenings they found their own entertainment and at weekends the local pubs were busy. H.P. White in his book *Forgotten Railways: South East England* recalls a letter written to a farmer which read: 'I have come hopping with you for the last twenty years and would like to come again. As you well know I've just had my tenth child – the local air seems to agree with me!'

During the early 1950s well over 4,000 hoppers and some 23,000 visitors travelled in 56 special trains but numbers were beginning to fall. Rising living standards and paid holidays had their effect and some were now coming by car or van.

Hops were not the only worthwhile traffic on the branch line. There was much freight to be carried with coal, fertilisers and groceries coming into the area and grain, fruit and hops being railed outwards. In later years over a million pot plants left Hawkhurst annually, mostly destined for Woolworths' stores.

Other sources of traffic to the area were the boarding schools of Benenden and Cranbrook. Benenden was usually served by a special train to and from Charing Cross often of six corridor coaches hauled by an E1 or D1 class 4-4-0 locomotive. Although boys from Cranbrook School had to be content with service trains, sometimes lengthened to four coaches. At end-of-term time, the quantities of trunks and other school items frequently reached such proportions that numerous utility vans were needed. The last special train to Benenden School left Charing Cross at 2.46 pm on 2nd May 1961, powered by D1 class locomotive no 31749, just six weeks before closure of the line.

After the Second World War traffic fell away dramatically. Hops were soon to be taken by road to Paddock Wood and market produce went by road all the way to London. Coal remained a useful traffic and the pot plants from local nurseries to Woolworths remained faithful throughout the last years bringing in freight receipts of around £1,000 a week. The plants were loaded at Hawkhurst to be taken on the last up train of the day to Tonbridge, possibly picking up further despatches at Horsmonden from a fruit-packing station. The busiest time was the week before Mothering Sunday when a special train was required.

The end finally came on 12th June 1961. Traffic had reduced to a trickle and the closure was only too predictable. Today the villages on the old Hawkhurst line continue to grow in size. Many folk remember the railway that served the area for almost 70 years and some still bemoan its loss.

The area that was once Hawkhurst station became a site for the Kent Woodware Co whose operations covered the entire area. The goods and engine shed remained and were put to good use. The original steps up from the road are still there and a familiar Southern Railway cast iron notice faces visitors. The signal box has been well preserved. The proprietor of Kent Woodware, a keen railway enthusiast, ensures to this day that the signal box receives 'a good coat of paint every other year'.

The Hawkhurst line was worked by steam all its life taking its passengers through some of the most delightful scenery. Today the local folk must be content with only a few relics to remind them of the past. But if, when walking at night, they hear the sound of a fox or owl they can perhaps imagine it is the distant whistle of an H class tank locomotive going about its business in a nearby siding.

Locomotive no 31500 arrives at Hawkhurst station, 1960. After closure in 1961 the station site became Kent Woodware where the signal box has been painstakingly preserved to this day. (R.K. Blencowe)

14
The Kent & East Sussex Light Railway

Locomotive AIX 'Terrier' 0-6-0T no 3 (later BR no 32670), built in 1872, photographed at Robertsbridge on 19th June 1948. A branch line from Robertsbridge to Headcorn via Tenterden was completed in 1905. (John H. Meredith)

A visitor to the Kent & East Sussex Railway (KESR) cannot fail to see the enthusiasm by which the present-day line is making progress. This well known project, originally one of the Colonel Stephens railways, runs trains today from Tenterden Town station as far as Bodiam which was reached in April 2000. At Bodiam visitors can enjoy the nearby castle, built in 1385 and described as 'one of the most famous and evocative castles in Britain'.

First proposals for a line to Tenterden came in the mid-19th

Bodiam station before closure of the branch in 1961. Nearby Bodiam Castle, which dates back to 1385, has always been an attraction for visitors over the years. (R.K. Blencowe)

century when the SER considered that its Ashford to Hastings line should pass through Tenterden but, when built a year later, a route through Appledore was chosen. Numerous plans were put forward in the years that followed linking Tenterden with either Headcorn or Paddock Wood, but none of these materialised. A more speculative idea to link Headcorn and Tenterden by a roadside tramway in 1872 also came to nothing.

It was not until 1896 that serious steps were taken to give Tenterden the railway it wanted. A group of local citizens proposed a line to be built from the town to Robertsbridge on the Tonbridge to Hastings line. Called the Rother Valley Railway, it was authorised in the same year. A Light Railway Order was obtained shortly afterwards making use of a new Act which reduced costs for the comparatively small concern. Construction was supervised by Holman F. Stephens who became General Manager in 1899 and Managing Director in 1900. Holman Stephens was promoted to Lieutenant-Colonel during the First World War and became known subsequently as 'Colonel

A well-worn sign reminds passers-by of the Rother Valley Railway (altered to KESR in 1904) and Colonel H. F. Stephens from earlier days. This picture was taken at Rolvenden in June 1948. (John H. Meredith)

Stephens', famous for his minor railway projects.

The first goods train ran on 26th March 1900 and passenger services followed on 2nd April. Apparently the first Tenterden terminus was not immediately popular since it was some 2 miles from the town centre (sited where Rolvenden station is today) and on the opening day only 60 people turned up for the first train at 7.30 am. It was not until 1903 that Tenterden got a more conveniently sited station at its present location. When it opened on 16th March the town celebrated. The inaugural train arrived to the accompaniment of a brass band and in the presence of Holman Stephens, various dignitaries and 300 school children. A large marquee had been erected in the yard.

A further Light Railway Order was obtained the same year for an extension to the SER Tonbridge–Ashford line at Headcorn and another order the following year changed the name of the company to the Kent & East Sussex Light Railway. So the KESR finally took shape in a line from Robertsbridge to be routed over the river Rother beyond Northiam and then via Tenterden to

Biddenden station on the Headcorn extension of the KESR soon after its opening in 1905. (Lens of Sutton Collection)

Robertsbridge station, c1938, where passengers changed for KESR trains. Ex-SECR P class locomotive 1556 has arrived from Headcorn with a selection of mixed coaches. (S.C. Townroe/R.K. Blencowe)

Headcorn. There were 13 stations on the route which included Junction Road Halt. This was opened eight months later than the others to serve (it claimed) Hawkhurst which was 4 miles away.

A further line was agreed in 1906 to extend the KESR from Headcorn to Maidstone and land was purchased in anticipation. But the company had insufficient funds to embark on such an expensive venture, which included the problem of crossing Sutton Valence Hill. The idea was abandoned and the land north of Headcorn was sold.

During the First World War the KESR acquired a horse-drawn omnibus to serve passengers from Tenterden Town station and this was used until 1922. When the railways were nationalised in 1948 the bus was found at the back of a shed and now it stands, gloriously restored, in the National Railway Museum, York.

Robertsbridge station on the main Tonbridge to Hastings line. On the right the bay which once served trains on the Kent & East Sussex Light Railway to Tenterden and Headcorn. (Anthony Rispoli)

Frittenden Road Halt which closed to regular passenger traffic in January 1954. (Lens of Sutton Collection)

Increasing losses were being incurred and a railbus was introduced as an economy measure. It was made from two Ford road buses linked back to back and fitted with flanged metal wheels in place of normal road wheels. This proved successful and a second set was introduced in 1924. A similar unit built by Shefflex Motors Ltd was in use by 1929. The first Ford set lasted only a few years but the second set and the Shefflex unit lasted until the late 1930s.

Colonel Stephens died in 1931 and within a year the branch was insolvent. The Colonel's assistant, Mr W.H. Austen, was appointed Official Receiver and, despite difficulties, he succeeded in running the railway for a further 16 years. During that time a highlight was the use of the locomotive *Northiam* which in 1937 was sent to the Basingstoke & Alton Light Railway for the making of the film *Oh! Mr Porter* starring Will Hay. To play the part of *Gladstone* a section of the cab was removed and a spiked chimney was added. On its return to Rolvenden, the engine was restored but saw little further service.

During the Second World War the line played an important

134

TRAVEL IN SAFETY ACROSS COUNTRY
AWAY FROM THE DUSTY AND CROWDED ROADS

KENT & EAST SUSSEX RAILWAY

To
**NORTHIAM,
BECKLEY,
SANDHURST,
EWHURST,
BODIAM** and
STAPLECROSS.

To
**WITTERSHAM,
ROLVENDEN,
TENTERDEN,
HIGH HALDEN,
BIDDENDEN** and
FRITTENDEN.

FIVE MINUTES' WALK FROM BODIAM STATION.

Omnibus Service in connection
to Maidstone, Cranbrook,
Benenden, Peasmarsh & Rye.

*Harriers and Coursing throughout
the District.*

**BOATING and FISHING on
THE RIVER ROTHER**

*Special Terms to Pleasure
and Picnic Parties
Good Hotel Accommodation.*

NORTHIAM MARKET alternate Wednesdays.

Golf Links at Tenterden.

Connection with Southern Railway at Robertsbridge and Headcorn

Easy and Cheap Access to Bodiam Castle (Open to Public daily except Sundays)

SEPT. 26th, 1927, and until further notice

DOWN TRAINS. Week Days Only.

UP TRAINS. Week Days Only.

MOTOR RAIL CARS ONE CLASS ONLY. ONLY HAND LUGGAGE ALLOWED.

SPECIAL SERVICE ON BANK HOLIDAYS

On Wednesdays, Cheap Return Tickets will be issued to London from
Tenterden Town, Rolvenden, Wittersham Road, Northiam, and Bodiam, *via*
Robertsbridge.

Also Tenterden Town, High Halden Road, and Biddenden, *via* Headcorn.

Daily Cheap Return Tickets will be issued to
HASTINGS, BEXHILL, TUNBRIDGE WELLS,
TONBRIDGE and ASHFORD.

See Small Handbills.

September, 1927.
DAVID ALLEN & SONS, Ltd., London and Belfast

Managing Director's Office, Tonbridge, Kent.

H. F. STEPHENS, Managing Director.

role with railway guns based on the KESR tracks. An 86 ton 9.2 inch Mk 13 gun was located at Rolvenden station from February 1941 to August 1944. Its companion was named *SM Cleeve* and was placed at Wittersham Road. Both belonged to the No 4 (Suffolk) Super-Heavy Railway Battery RA. Only one shell was fired in anger and this was when one of the guns was based at Folkestone before its installation at the KESR. In October 1940 a number of German torpedo boats were seen cruising at a range of nearly 14 miles by a clifftop observer. Fog made cross bearings difficult and a 385 lb shell landed beyond the boats causing them to scatter towards the French coast. The enemy need not have concerned itself for the gun had derailed itself and presented no further threat. In June 1941 a practice shot was fired at Wittersham Road causing a further derailment and the shattering of numerous windows. Two days later further shots were fired in practice without incident with the guns remaining valuable defence weapons.

In January 1948 the KESR became part of British Railways Southern Region. An inspection of the track revealed many deficiencies and of the nine coaches checked only two were retained and many trucks were scrapped. In spite of this, the KESR survived a further five years and conditions improved for a time. On 4th January 1954 passenger traffic from Robertsbridge to Headcorn was withdrawn. The line from Robertsbridge to Tenterden remained open for goods with seasonal use by hop-pickers' specials, the testing of diesel locomotives and occasional passenger specials. The section to Headcorn was dismantled in 1955. In July 1961 the Locomotive Club of Great Britain organised a seven-coach special hauled by 'Terrier' 0-6-0Ts nos 32662 and 32670 which proved to be the last passenger train along the line under BR ownership. On the following day all services along the line ceased.

Although the track northwards from Tenterden to Headcorn has been lifted the line is not difficult to trace. Tenterden St Michael's Halt has gone but it was sited at the lower end of Orchard Road and St Michael's tunnel still remains beneath a lane. High Halden Road station building survived the closure to be used by a farm to store potatoes. Biddenden station remained in good trim, used as a private dwelling with the goods yard

Locomotive 0-6-0T no 32678 with passenger coach arrives at Tenterden from Robertsbridge in the 1950s. The line closed to passengers in 1954 remaining open for freight until 1961. (John H. Meredith)

Wittersham Road station, c1938, which closed to passengers in 1954. When reopened by the KESR in 1977 a station building was acquired from Borth on the Cambrian Coast line. (Lens of Sutton)

KESR trains reached Bodiam station in April 2000. Diesel railcars await return to Tenterden. (Author)

A Norwegian class 21c locomotive 2-6-0 no 376, built 1919, runs round a train at Bodiam in July 2001. (Arthur Tayler)

becoming a garden. The last intermediate station before Headcorn, Frittenden Road, was put to use as a farm building.

The Kent & East Sussex Railway Preservation Society (later reconstituted as the Tenterden Railway Co Ltd) came into being soon after closure of the line. By 1974 a section of track had been reopened and trains were running from Tenterden Town to Rolvenden. Restoring the bridge across Newmill Channel proved a major problem with the girders and abutments badly corroded and scoured and a new bridge had to be built. Apart from this the river banks had to be raised to prevent flooding. Little wonder that the area many years ago was part of an inland waterway system with many small ports.

Thanks to a second-hand bridge from Aylesford provided by Kent County Council and the help of a job creation programme, the replacement bridge was completed by November 1976. Trains reached Wittersham Road by March 1977 but it was a further 15 months of intensive work before a platform and building could be completed. This was done with a collection of items from Heathfield on the Cuckoo Line, Cranbrook, Deal junction and even as far away as Borth on the Cambrian Coast line which provided the station building.

Northiam station was reached in June 1990 and in April 2000 trains reached Bodiam, 100 years to the day since trains first steamed along the track. The event was celebrated with Sir Alastair Morton, Strategic Rail Authority Chairman, officiating at a grand ceremony to mark the completion of the 'Millennium Extension'. With so much hard work and enthusiasm, it is not surprising that the KESR has been called 'The Line that Refused to Die'.

15
Lines To The Collieries And A Preserved Line

The potential of coal in Kent was first considered in the 1850s although no firm action was taken until some 40 years later. Geologists drew attention to the possibility and a paper to the Geological Society in 1855 referred to 'possible coal measures beneath the South East Part of England'. Borings were made at Battle in Sussex between 1872 and 1875 but, as luck had it, no coal was found.

The first successful boring was brought about more by chance. In the late 1870s construction was in hand to build a tunnel under the Channel although progress was stopped in 1882 by the Board of Trade. Nevertheless use was made of the Shakespeare Cliff site at Dover since a further boring made in 1890 found coal at 1,100 ft below the surface.

Still no sensational developments followed throughout the county, probably because the Dover pit was so prone to flooding as to be uneconomical. However, the find gave the stimulus to look elsewhere. Over the next decade quantities of coal were located throughout the east of the county and mining began in earnest. Since a number of pits were isolated from main railway lines a local inquiry was held at the County Hotel, Canterbury, to consider a network of new lines to cover the area. In this way the East Kent Light Railway (EKLR) was born, thought by some to become one of Colonel Stephens' less successful ventures. Initially the enthusiasm was there and many felt that Kent could be termed a 'second Lancashire'.

At the meeting a network of lines was proposed with two main routes forming a letter Y with its extremities near Canterbury and at Richborough Port and the base at Shepherdswell on the SER line from Dover to Canterbury. The hub of the system was to be at Eastry and it was considered that Richborough could be developed to concentrate traffic for export.

A Light Railway Order for single-track working was granted on 19th June 1911, which included numerous sidings to pits although some of these lines were never built. The first line to open was from Shepherdswell to Wingham Colliery, 6 miles beyond Eastry, which began with freight traffic only in November 1912 with passenger traffic following in October 1916. Subsequent Railway Orders followed to various pits where in a number of cases some shafts were sunk and surface buildings completed but no coal was ever produced. Lines worked included Guilford, served by a 2 mile branch southwards from Eythorne, and Hammill beyond Eastry. This latter working eventually became a brickyard. A worthwhile pit was opened in 1913 at Tilmanstone and it was not long before a short branch reached the area from Eythorne.

A major engineering work during construction of the line was Golgotha tunnel between Shepherdswell and Eythorne. Initially a temporary line was built round Golgotha Hill and later, when

Saddle tank locomotive 0-6-0 no 7 plus mixed passenger set at Sandwich Road on the EKLR in September 1928. The passenger service from Eastry to Sandwich Road opened in 1925 but only goods trains reached the terminus at Richborough Port since the bridge over the Stour often flooded at high tide! (Lens of Sutton Collection)

the tunnel had been completed, it was removed. Colonel Stephens inserted an arched brick roof in the tunnel sufficient for double track but had only excavated enough below for a single line so that costs for any eventual doubling would be much reduced. Such was the optimism in those early days that, for much of the route, land for double track had been purchased. There were even boasts about an extension as far as London.

Despite these high feelings, it was to be very much a light railway with speed restricted to 25 mph and reductions according to gradient. Also, taking advantage of the relaxation in requirements for costly equipment permitted by the Act, the EKLR provided the simplest of stations, short platforms edged with timber or brick and a 'bus stop' type of shelter. Control of the trains was by telephone between block posts and there were few fixed signals. Ideas of through trains to London, or even Canterbury, were optimistic indeed!

In 1916 Eastry to Sandwich Road, not far from Richborough Port, opened as a mineral line and this prompted the EKLR to consider that after the war coal could be exported by this means. During the First World War the port was used for military traffic to supplement Dover and Folkestone and it was reached by a siding off the SECR Minster–Deal line. After the war in 1918 the harbour was virtually out of use and Colonel Stephens' hopes of a great new port with cross-Channel services came to nothing.

In 1925 a passenger service opened from Eastry to Sandwich Road (on the A257) which the EKLR hopefully considered would serve the town of Sandwich over a mile away. A track finally reached Richborough in 1929 completed with capital provided by the Southern Railway but it was used for goods only. Passengers never reached Richborough because there were restrictions over Stour Bridge which had been built with a fixed span resting on temporary wooden piers. Apparently it was not clear if the bridge, with a height given as 24 ft 8 in, was above sea level at high tide. So any train comprising passenger and goods traffic combined left its coaches behind at Sandwich Road and went on to Richborough to collect or deliver any freight.

During the 1920s the fortunes of the EKLR improved. Freight tonnage for 1927 was 222,320. The Southern Railway took an interest and injected cash and a colliery at Snowdown, previ-

Poison Cross Halt on the Eastry to Sandwich Road section of the EKLR lasted only three years, closing in 1928. The line remained open for goods traffic to Richborough until 1949. (Lens of Sutton Collection)

ously closed, was reopened. Had it not been for a depression in trade, the changes from coal to oil and from rail to road traffic, the EKLR may well have prospered.

As far as passenger trains were concerned these were hardly a success. Apart from a Pickering-built vestibule car from 1912, most coaches were the four or six-wheel type more or less discarded by their previous owners, the LSWR, the North London Railway and the SECR. In Edwin Course's book, *The Railways of Southern England: Independent and Light Railways*, there is an amusing account of a mishap to a morning train from Shepherdswell up to a pit. Apparently the last carriage jostled off the rails to become disconnected, while the rest of the train 'chuffed off happily along to the colliery leaving a carriage-load of disgruntled men and boys behind.' With such appalling standards of maintenance to the rolling stock and track, it was hardly surprising the line never succeeded.

In 1925 a stretch of line opened from Wingham Colliery to Canterbury Road. There had been ideas that this would eventually extend to Canterbury but this never happened.

Wingham station, the end of the EKLR colliery line. There were plans to extend this branch to Canterbury but it never happened. (Lens of Sutton Collection)

Although such a move would have increased workmen's traffic on the EKLR, the Southern Railway was not at all keen. Firstly it would undoubtedly have lost traffic from the main line to Shepherdswell and secondly, the SR was soon to acquire a substantial shareholding interest in the East Kent Road Car Co.

The first reverse came in 1928 when the passenger service from Eastry to Sandwich Road closed. The decision came as no surprise bearing in mind that the EKLR had developed a reputation of 'failing to run where people wanted to go'. Two years later, in an effort to cut costs, the East Kent Colliery Co, which owned Tilmanstone, took further trade away from the EKLR by building an aerial cableway to the eastern arm of Dover Harbour where large hoppers stored the coal. As it happened it was little used and was idle by 1939, but it was no encouragement to the prospects of the EKLR.

During the Second World War, rail guns were used on EKLR tracks, being kept at various locations including Shepherdswell, Eythorne and Staple. When war ended, the management did their best to smarten the line by repairing buildings and old rolling stock. A number of vehicles were broken up for scrap and

144

several locomotives were stored at Shepherdswell to await a doubtful fate.

When passenger traffic from Shepherdswell to Canterbury Road ceased on 30th October 1948, it was the end of all passenger traffic on the EKLR and the first line to be axed following nationalisation. Goods traffic between Eastry and Richborough closed in October 1949 and the Canterbury Road section followed in July 1950. A year later Eythorne to Eastry closed. All that remained was the short stretch from the main line to Eythorne and Tilmanstone Colliery which was worked by a diesel shunting engine making several trips a day.

In March 1968 people living near the surviving stretch were no doubt surprised to see a main line train with a diesel at each end covering the route to Tilmanstone. This was an 'Invicta Rail Tour' run by the Locomotive Club of Great Britain. After climbing to Golgotha the train went on to one of the colliery sidings where, for some, lunch was served in the restaurant car.

A Dover Priory to Victoria via Canterbury fast working train stops at Shepherdswell, October 2002. The rail link between Shepherdswell and Tilmanstone Colliery is now severed although track to the colliery survives, part of it in use by the preserved East Kent Light Railway. (Anthony Rispoli)

145

These level-crossing gates mark where tracks, once busy with coal traffic, went through to Tilmanstone Colliery. The last train left Tilmanstone in March 1984. (Anthony Rispoli)

Quite a contradiction from the rackety four or six-wheeled coaches of years back.

Trains no longer run to Tilmanstone Colliery (now closed) but much of the line remains in situ. The last train left Tilmanstone at 12.55 on 1st March 1984, hauling seven coke wagons bound for Tyneside. Elsewhere lines were lifted and buildings demolished, and little remains. A good reminder of those early days can be achieved by a visit to the Bluebell Railway at Sheffield Park in Sussex to see the 4-4-2T Adams Radial no 488 which from 1919 to 1946 served as EKLR locomotive no 5.

A Line Preserved

Golgotha tunnel on today's preserved East Kent Light Railway between Shepherdswell and Eythorne. It was originally built to accommodate double track but only single track was ever completed. (Anthony Rispoli)

In 1993 The East Kent Light Railway Society obtained the Light Railway Order which allowed regular passenger trains to run on the East Kent lines after an absence of over 40 years. The Society was formed in 1985 with the intention of preserving the remaining section of line, but it was not until 1989 that volunteers were able to start the massive task of clearing the large amounts of vegetation that had covered the tracks since closure. Since that time the Society has transformed the station area and its surroundings at Shepherdswell. A replica of the original station building and platform has been built, access roads and car parks have been laid and toilets and picnic areas provided.

A train arrives at Eythorne station on the preserved East Kent Light Railway, August 2002. There are hopes that at a future date trains might reach Tilmanstone. (Anthony Rispoli)

At Shepherdswell the Society has adopted the atmosphere of the railway as it would have been in Colonel Stephens' day, hence no large buildings or major structures. Visitors can enjoy viewing a large collection of rolling stock, a small exhibition and a museum which shows how the East Kent Light Railway looked in its heyday.

The railway today runs from Shepherdswell to Eythorne, a 4 mile round trip. There are hopes that at some future date trains will run as far as the former Tilmanstone Colliery. Track is being relaid in places and there is no shortage of enthusiasm among the helpers. But much needs to be done.

148

16
The Channel Tunnel –
Past And Present

Overlooking Cheriton where today's Channel Tunnel trains enter on their journey to France and Belgium. First fare-paying passenger trains began in December 1994. (Anthony Rispoli)

The idea of a Channel Tunnel was first conceived in 1802 when a French mining engineer, Albert Mathieu, considered linking Britain and the Continent with a tunnel from Cap Gris Nez to a bay near Folkestone. The following year, an Englishman called Mottray thought up a plan to build an immersible steel tube to lay on the Channel bed. However, such plans were soon vetoed on the British side when it was seen that Napoleon was considering the scheme to further his invasion plans of Britain.

In the 1870s, when thoughts of war between the two countries were forgotten, the idea was taken more seriously. On 11th May 1875 the SER agreed to make a grant of £20,000 towards trials to test the possibilities of a tunnel provided that the rival LCDR did the same. Since the SER appeared to gain most from such an enterprise, it was to be expected that the LCDR would remain uncommitted. By the late 1870s some work was in progress near Shakespeare Cliff at Dover. This made little progress and was halted in 1882 for 'reasons of defence'. The generals of the day imagined a French army marching through the tunnel unimpeded.

In the year 1923, Sir Percy Tempest, then chief engineer for the Channel Tunnel project, published a memorandum. Sir Percy estimated the cost at £29 million and assessed that boring machines would provide a tunnel 12 ft in diameter at a rate of 120 ft a day. It was suggested that boring machines should start simultaneously from each side and they would meet in 2½ years.

Eurostar on a Waterloo to Brussels Channel Tunnel service passes through Tonbridge on 9th September 1999. (Arthur Tayler)

Allowing for all other work entailed, the project was expected to take 4½ years.

Again the idea was shelved and not taken up seriously again until well after nationalisation of the railways in 1948. In 1964 there was agreement in principle on both sides for a rail tunnel from Cheriton to Sangatte near Calais but it was not until February 1974 that work started on a service road through Shakespeare Cliff. Engineers then commenced a road tunnel intended to reach the alignment of the planned rail tunnel.

However, the respective Governments had still not ratified the Treaty, money had been running short and there had been many objections. In early 1975 the companies involved abandoned the project although the works remained and could be seen by passengers from passing trains at Lower Shakespeare Cliff. The entrance had been lined with concrete slabs and a £500,000 laser beam boring 'mole' had stood in the tunnel awaiting a further attempt. A trial bore had reached 250 metres. Many more slabs stood unused on the land 'platform' – the same area that was

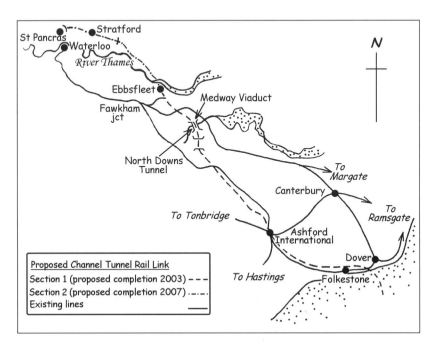

created in 1843 from 'spoils' following the blasting of the chalk face when the Dover to Folkestone railway line was built.

Today's Channel Tunnel Rail Link (CTRL), which opened to fare-paying passengers in December 1994, is described as one of Europe's biggest infrastructure projects to date. The tunnel consists of three interconnecting tubes comprising one rail track each way and a service tunnel. The length of the tunnel is 31 miles, 23 of which are under water. Its average depth is 150 feet under the seabed and the Channel crossing time for Eurostar is only 20 minutes. It is claimed that the volume of rubble removed from the tunnel is three times greater than that of the Cheops Pyramid, the largest in Egypt. It has increased the size of Britain by 90 acres and is equivalent to 68 football fields!

Completion of Section 1 (46 miles from the UK end of the tunnel to Fawkham junction on the existing Chatham to Swanley line) is expected by the end of 2003. It is calculated that more than 25 million man-hours are being worked to complete this project which includes a newly dug North Downs tunnel just south of Chatham. Stage 2 will extend the CTRL to London, St Pancras and it is planned to open in 2007.

The Channel Tunnel has had, and is still having, its controversial moments. But it has totally transformed our conception of cross-Channel traffic. When in 1881 Sir Edward Watkin, Chairman of the SER, stood on a beach at Dungeness envisaging crossing the Channel, he little envisaged the present outcome. How he would have liked to be involved in such happenings.

Conclusion

The decline of many Kent lines began in the 1920s. Buses were increasingly providing a more flexible service than the trains and in addition road haulage was on the increase. An early casualty was a line from Margate Sands to Ramsgate Town, including the short branch to Ramsgate Harbour, both of which closed in July 1926.

More lines quickly followed. The Elham Valley line closed to passengers in June 1947. With the number of passengers averaging daily about a dozen in each direction, the end was inevitable. The branch from Queenborough to Leysdown closed in December 1950. In December 1951 traffic on the line from Sandling Junction to Hythe came to an end and in August 1953 the Gravesend West branch line closed to passenger services. The Kent & East Sussex Railway was closed to passenger services by British Rail in 1954.

Meantime changes were taking place which were to materially affect the railways and their future. With living standards rising and paid holidays becoming an accepted condition of work, people were willing to live further from their place of work. Electricity was becoming more freely available and, with the coalfields of the North no longer vital to industry, people were migrating southwards. The South East became a popular area bringing with it the need to provide extensive suburban rail services between the capital and the surrounding districts.

Electric trains did not reach Kent until after the 'grouping' in 1923. Powers had been obtained as early as 1903 but the necessary capital had not then been available. In August 1926 it was announced that the Eastern section would be electrified on the DC third rail system. Orpington, Bromley North, Addiscombe, Hayes and Dartford were reached in the same year. Further electrification followed in Kent but progress was slow. Sevenoaks (Tubs Hill) was reached in 1935 but lines to Maidstone were not electrified until July 1939.

Benefits, however, were immediate. Track layouts were changed to accommodate the new trains, signalling systems were modernised and platforms were reorganised. Timetables were altered to give more frequent services at regular intervals, considerably increased during peak travel periods.

The war effectively wrecked the finances of the railways which were to be saved by nationalisation in 1948. With government subsidies involved it was inevitable that 'rationalisation' processes would follow. Management of the main line railways was delegated by the British Transport Commission to the Railway Executive with the Southern Region taking charge of all lines in the south. But progress to commence capital investment programmes was slow due to material shortages. In addition integration with other forms of transport, a declared aim of nationalisation, made little headway.

In 1953 there were changes. A Transport Act aimed at de-centralisation dissolved the Railway Executive and from January 1955 the Southern Region was controlled by a Board, responsible to the Commission, but with considerable freedom to determine its own actions. Three Divisions were created, the 'South Eastern', 'South Western' and 'Central'.

Despite optimistic plans for redevelopment, freight traffic was still on the decline and the railways were becoming more dependent on passenger traffic. By the early 1960s, the government's attitude had hardened. In a further Transport Act of 1962, it was clear that commercial viability was considered a more important factor than providing a service to the public. In 1963 the Transport Commission was dissolved and a new Railways Board created. At the same time, the Minister of Transport appointed the Stedeford Group to look at the future of the railways. The findings were not published but one of its members was Dr Richard Beeching (later Lord Beeching), a name that was to become very well known in the years to come.

In March 1963 proposals were made in a report which became popularly known as the 'Beeching Plan'. Basically the idea was to keep lines considered suitable to rail traffic and give up the remainder. It had been calculated that one third of the rail system in Britain carried only one per cent of the total traffic! The report was considered disappointing in ignoring the potential of many Southern lines, particularly related to electrification. Also by planning the closure of many freight depots, it was thought the report failed to foresee the future of container traffic in the region. Line singling, 'bus stop' type stations for economy and the use of diesel electric locomotives were other aspects considered overlooked at the time.

At the present time continuing financial losses on the railways appear inevitable. Perhaps there is comfort in the fact that further widespread closures on the scale previously suffered would be politically unacceptable today. Presumably government subsidies will continue and will, no doubt, increase in the years to come.

From the days of Kent's early turnpikes and tollgates, time has taken us through the canal age to the railway age. 'Railway mania' is now well behind us and we are back to the roads once again with cars and motorways a part of present-day life. Yet already many roads and motorways are quite inadequate for the task intended, with lorries continually increasing in weight and the volume of traffic reaching ever higher proportions. Surely those who closed down so many of our branch lines have much to answer for.

It is difficult at the present time to foresee the railway's future. One of the main disadvantages is that this is in the hands of politicians. Sadly the days have gone when the railways provided an efficient service throughout and when railway employees could take a real pride in the job.

Opening and Final Closure Dates of Lines to Regular Passenger Traffic

Line	Opened	Final Closure
Canterbury & Whitstable	1830	1931
Ramsgate Town to Margate Sands	1846	1926
Queenborough to Sheerness Dock	1860	1922
Ramsgate Harbour branch	1863	1926
Tunbridge Wells West to Groombridge	1866	1985
Sandling Junction to Hythe	1874	1951
Hythe to Sandgate	1874	1931
Queenborough to Queenborough Pier *1	1876	1914
Dunton Green to Westerham	1881	1961
Appledore to Lydd	1881	1967
Hoo junction to Sharnal Street	1882	1961
Sharnal Street to Port Victoria *2	1882	1961
Lydd to Dungeness	1884	1937
Lydd to New Romney	1884	1967
Fawkham junction to Gravesend West	1886	1953
Cheriton junction to Barham	1887	1947
Barham to Harbledown junction	1889	1947
Strood to Chatham Central	1892	1911
Paddock Wood to Hawkhurst	1893	1961
Robertsbridge to Rolvenden	1900	1954
Queenborough to Leysdown	1901	1950
Rolvenden to Tenterden Town *3	1903	1954
Tenterden Town to Headcorn	1905	1954
Sittingbourne & Kemsley Light Railway *4	from 1906	1969
East Kent Light Railway *5	from 1912	1948
Stoke junction to Allhallows-on-Sea	1932	1961

*1 Temporarily reopened 1932
*2 Grain Crossing to Port Victoria closed earlier on 4th September 1951
*3 Section reopened in 1947 by the KESR Preservation Society
*4 Section preserved by the S&KLR in 1971
*5 Section from Shepherdswell to Eythorne opened by preserved EKLR in 1995

Please note that:
Junction implies a railway station
junction means where railway lines meet.

Bibliography

In compiling *Lost Railways of Kent*, I have referred to numerous sources, many now out of print, which include the following and which can be recommended for further reading:

Carley, James *The Turnpikes of Kent* (Kent County Library)

Course, Dr Edwin *The Railway of Southern England: The Main Lines; The Secondary and Branch Lines; Independent and Light Railways* (B.T. Batsford)

Gould, David *Westerham Valley Railway* (Oakwood Press)

Green, Simon B. *The KESR Guide* (Buffer Stop Books, Tenterden)

Hadfield, Charles *The Canals of South and South East England* (David & Charles)

Hart, Brian *The Elham Valley Line* (Wild Swan Publications)

Kidner, R.W. *The SECR* (Oakwood Press)

Marshall, C.F. Dendy, revised by Kidner, R.W. *History of the Southern Railway* (Ian Allen Ltd)

Maxted, I. *The Canterbury & Whistable Railway* (Oakwood Press)

Pallant, Nick *The Gravesend West Branch* (Oakwood Press)

Ratcliffe, A.R.L. *Bygone SE Steam, Volume 4: Closed Branch Lines* (Rochester Press, Chatham)

Scott Morgan, John *The Colonel Stephens Railways* (David & Charles)

White, H.P. *A Regional History of the Railways of Great Britain, Volume 2: Southern England* and *Forgotten Railways: South East England* (David & Charles)

Reference has also been made to websites as under. These can usefully be referred to for additional information.

http://londonse.topcities.com Anthony Rispoli *The Railways of London & The South East*

www.transport-of-delight.com John F. Bradshaw *UK Stations and Signal Boxes*

Index